INTERNATIONAL ENERG

CREATING MARKETS FOR
ENERGY TECHNOLOGIES

INTERNATIONAL ENERGY AGENCY
9, rue de la Fédération,
75739 Paris, cedex 15, France

The International Energy Agency (IEA) is an autonomous body which was established in November 1974 within the framework of the Organisation for Economic Co-operation and Development (OECD) to implement an international energy programme.

It carries out a comprehensive programme of energy co-operation among twenty-six* of the OECD's thirty Member countries. The basic aims of the IEA are:

- to maintain and improve systems for coping with oil supply disruptions;

- to promote rational energy policies in a global context through co-operative relations with non-member countries, industry and international organisations;

- to operate a permanent information system on the international oil market;

- to improve the world's energy supply and demand structure by developing alternative energy sources and increasing the efficiency of energy use;

- to assist in the integration of environmental and energy policies.

* *IEA Member countries: Australia, Austria, Belgium, Canada, the Czech Republic, Denmark, Finland, France, Germany, Greece, Hungary, Ireland, Italy, Japan, the Republic of Korea, Luxembourg, the Netherlands, New Zealand, Norway, Portugal, Spain, Sweden, Switzerland, Turkey, the United Kingdom, the United States. The European Commission also takes part in the work of the IEA.*

ORGANISATION FOR
ECONOMIC CO-OPERATION
AND DEVELOPMENT

Pursuant to Article 1 of the Convention signed in Paris on 14th December 1960, and which came into force on 30th September 1961, the Organisation for Economic Co-operation and Development (OECD) shall promote policies designed:

- to achieve the highest sustainable economic growth and employment and a rising standard of living in Member countries, while maintaining financial stability, and thus to contribute to the development of the world economy;

- to contribute to sound economic expansion in Member as well as non-member countries in the process of economic development; and

- to contribute to the expansion of world trade on a multilateral, non-discriminatory basis in accordance with international obligations.

The original Member countries of the OECD are Austria, Belgium, Canada, Denmark, France, Germany, Greece, Iceland, Ireland, Italy, Luxembourg, the Netherlands, Norway, Portugal, Spain, Sweden, Switzerland, Turkey, the United Kingdom and the United States. The following countries became Members subsequently through accession at the dates indicated hereafter: Japan (28th April 1964), Finland (28th January 1969), Australia (7th June 1971), New Zealand (29th May 1973), Mexico (18th May 1994), the Czech Republic (21st December 1995), Hungary (7th May 1996), Poland (22nd November 1996), the Republic of Korea (12th December 1996) and Slovakia (28th September 2000). The Commission of the European Communities takes part in the work of the OECD (Article 13 of the OECD Convention).

FOREWORD

Expanding markets for clean and efficient energy technologies is an effective policy pathway towards reducing greenhouse gas emissions and increasing energy security. But many promising technologies face cost hurdles or other obstacles to commercial deployment. Creating markets for the new technologies requires new initiatives.

At their 1999 meeting, IEA Energy Ministers "emphasised the need to mobilise public and private resources to deploy environmentally sound technologies globally". IEA's Committee on Energy Research and Technology subsequently initiated a project on lessons learned and best practices in technology deployment policies. A project group was set up by the IEA Secretariat to conduct the analysis. IEA governments and other partners provided case studies on successful deployment programmes. This book presents the findings of the project.

The context for the programmes varies from country to country. To generalise lessons learned, the cases are therefore analysed from three different perspectives. The Research, Development and Deployment perspective focuses on learning processes and learning investments to reduce cost and reach large-scale markets. The Market Barrier perspective applies economic analysis in order to understand the mechanisms impeding deployment of new technologies. The Market Transformation perspective considers the network of market actors and practical techniques to stimulate technological change. The key message is that the design and implementation of successful deployment programmes demands vision from all three perspectives.

Following their analysis, the project group at the IEA Secretariat arranged a workshop around the three perspectives in November 2001. Authors of case studies were joined by researchers and industry representatives. The participants confirmed and enlarged on the three-perspective framework. The project group's analysis and the workshop papers are the basis for this book.

Robert Priddle
Executive Director

ACKNOWLEDGEMENTS

The primary source of information for this book were the case studies which were provided by: David Beecy (US), Anna Engleryd (EU), Ken Friedman (US), P.V. Gilli (A), Charles Glaser (US), Wilfried Grasse (Solar PACES), Richard Karney (US), Keiichi Kawakami (J), Gudrun Knutsson (S), Martti Korkiakoski (SF), Vello Kuuskraa (US), Kees Kwant (NL), Jens H. Laustsen (DK), Anders Lewald (S), Gilles Mercier (CAN), Barbara McKee (US), Boris Papousek (A), Christian Rakos (A). Rainer Schneider (D), Richard Shock (UK), Willem Van Zanten (NL), Peter Versteegh (NL).

At the November 2001 workshop "Technologies Require Markets", Mel Kliman, Peter Lund and Leo Schrattenholzer analysed the case studies, each from one of the three perspectives. Their reports contributed to the chapters describing the perspectives. Other contributors to the workshop were: Lars Bergman, Graham Campbell, Ken Friedman, Jim Hansen, Phil Harrington, Winfrid Hoffman, Marc Ledbetter, Bengt-Åke Lundvall, Simon Minett, Francois Moisan, Hans Nilsson, Clas-Otto Wene.

Mel Kliman has acted as external editor-in-chief for this book, pulling the different pieces together into a narrative. The IEA Secretariat thanks the Norwegian Government for its financial support for the work on this publication.

The project group leading the work at the IEA Secretariat consisted of Maria Virdis (until September 2000), Clas-Otto Wene (since October 2000) and Hans Nilsson (since December 2000). Maria Virdis defined and collected the case studies. Hans Nilsson and Clas-Otto Wene developed the three-perspective framework, conducted the November 2001 workshop and provided analysis for this book.

TABLE OF CONTENTS

Foreword *3*

Acknowledgement *5*

*Executive Summary: Creating Markets for Energy
Technologies* *11*

*Chapter 1: In Search of a Comprehensive Approach
to Market Development Policy* *15*

Technology and Economic Change 15
Understanding Market Development Policy 16
Three Perspectives 18
What is to Come 20

Chapter 2: An Overview of the Case Studies *23*

End-use Technologies Ready for Use 26
   Energy Efficiency Best Practice 26
   Technology Procurement 28
   Other Building Sector Programmes 31
Renewable Energy Technologies 33
Fossil-based Technologies 36
Technology Transfer 38

*Chapter 3: A Research, Development
and Deployment Perspective* *41*

The Double Effect of Market Deployment 41
Two Types of Learning 46
Creating Conditions for Organisational Learning 47
Providing Opportunities for Technology Learning 53
Strategic Niche Market Management 58

Chapter 4: *A Market Barriers Perspective* **63**

Introduction 63

Market Barriers and Economic Analysis 64

   Market Failure in Relation to Typical Market Barriers 66

   Second-best Solutions to Market Failure 68

   Market Barriers in a Dynamic Setting 69

Applying Economic Analysis 71

   Performance Objectives 72

   Market Infrastructure 74

   Programme Efficiency and Success 75

Where to from here? 79

Chapter 5: *A Market Transformation Perspective* **81**

What is Market Transformation? 81

Doing Market Transformation 85

   Procurement Actions 93

   Strategic Niche Management 95

   Business Concept Innovation 98

Facing the Challenge 99

Chapter 6: *Tools for Policy Design* **101**

Analytical Tools 101

   Life-cycle Cost and Yield Calculations 102

   Experience Curves 104

   Using the Diffusion Model 106

Success has Many Faces 106

   Volume Growth 108

   Volume Growth and Price/Cost Trends 110

   Attribution of Impacts to Policy Measures 112

   Performance Improvements 115

   Benefit-Cost Analysis 116

   Summary Comments 117

Chapter 7: Looking at Policy-making from Multiple Perspectives 119

Policy Measures Viewed from Three Perspectives 120
Perspective-based Observations 122
    Barriers as Theories and Facts 124
    R&D as a Policy Tool 126
    Market Transformation 127
A simple Proposal for a More Comprehensive Perspective 128
Further Empirical Analysis 133

Chapter 8: Conclusions: What have we Learned? 137

Sources Used 141

Appendix: Case Diagnoses, Measures and Results 147

List of Figures and Tables

Figures

Figure 1.1. Putting Together an Overall Perspective on Technology
Market Development 20
Figure 3.1. Influences on the Learning System from Public Policies .. 43
Figure 3.2. Double-loop Learning 51
Figure 3.3. Thirty Years of Technology Learning 55
Figure 3.4. Making Photovoltaics Break Even 55
Figure 3.5. Interplay Between Niche Markets and the Experience Curve
for a Technology Challenging the Incumbent Technology
in the Market 60
Figure 5.1. Effect of Market Transformation on Product Performance .. 81
Figure 5.2. Developing Networks for Market Transformation 92
Figure 5.3. Technology Procurement Process 92
Figure 5.4. Bringing New Technology into the Market Through
a Controlled Experimentation Process 97
Figure 6.1. "Multiplication" of Yield on an Investment 104
Figure 6.2. Investments and Subsidies in PV-Roof Programme 105
Figure 6.3. Who will Buy and why? 107
Figure 6.4. Worldwide Sales of CFLs 109

Figure 6.5. Projected Growth of CFLs 111
Figure 6.6. Market Changes for PV Modules 1976-1996 113
Figure 6.7. Stages in a Market Introduction Process 113
Figure 6.8. EU Cold Appliances Sale by Energy Label 116
Figure 7.1. Differing Interpretations of a Deployment Study 121

Tables

Table 2.1. Deployment Policy Case Studies 25
Table 4.1. Types of Market Barriers and Measures that Can Alleviate
Them 65
Table 5.1. IEA Case Studies Categorised According to the Extent
Market Transformation Tools were Used 88
Table 5.2. Types of Market Actors Involved in Case Study Projects ... 91
Table 6.1. Increases in Yields on an Investment for Years of Useful
Life Longer than the Payback Time Required 103
Table 6.2. CFL Ownership in the European Union 110
Table 7.1 Differing Interpretations of Deployment Measures 123
Table 7.2. Operational Policy Objectives in Deployment Programmes
and their Characteristic Applications 130
Table 7.3. Operational Policy Objectives Related to Perspective-linked
Issues 132

List of Files on the Attached CD-ROM

Case Studies

Summaries of Case-Study Findings

Rapporteur 1

Mel Kliman, "Developing Markets for New Technologies: A Review of the Case Studies from the Market Barrier Perspective", paper presented to IEA Workshop, *Technologies Require Markets: Best Practices and Lessons Learned in Energy Technology Deployment Policies*, Paris 28-29 November 2001.

Rapporteur 2

Leo Schrattenholzer, "Analysing the Case Studies from the Perspective of the R&D and Deployment Model", paper presented to IEA Workshop, *Technologies Require Markets: Best Practices and Lessons Learned in Energy Technology Deployment Policies*, Paris 28-29 November 2001.

Rapporteur 3

Peter Lund, "Market Transformation Perspective and Involvement of Market Actors and Stakeholders in the IEA Case Studies", paper presented to IEA Workshop, *Technologies Require Markets: Best Practices and Lessons Learned in Energy Technology Deployment Policies*, Paris 28-29 November 2001.

EXECUTIVE SUMMARY: CREATING MARKETS FOR ENERGY TECHNOLOGIES

The development of markets for cleaner and more efficient energy technologies is at the centre of efforts in industrial societies to achieve a better fit between economic growth and environmental protection, and to deliver lasting energy security. Clean energy technologies will be the building blocks of a transformed energy system – a key component of the more sustainable economy we are seeking in the 21st century – but only if they can be made to perform at a level and a cost that society deems acceptable.

The technological and market developments required to transform the energy system will be conceived and implemented largely in the private sector. But success in this endeavour will not be determined exclusively by market forces. Governments that value the wider benefits of cleaner and more efficient energy technologies will work in partnership with market actors to ensure there are real opportunities for technologies to make the difficult transition from laboratory to market. This book is about the design and implementation of policies and programmes for that purpose.

Governments are motivated to assist not only because they have a responsibility for the pursuit of long-term societal goals and stewardship of the planet, but also because they understand that their policy settings help to determine whether markets develop and operate efficiently. Policymakers must therefore understand the markets concerned and they must have a highly developed capacity to mount effective programmes. In both cases experience is the best teacher.

For that reason IEA Member countries have come together to share their national experiences in technology deployment policy. The IEA has collected 22 studies of successful market development programmes. These case studies provide a wealth of information on the variety of programmes undertaken and the evolution of ideas in this policy area. Most importantly they inform us of the benefits of experience on the path to success in facilitating technology market development.

Because the value of the kind of information contained in the case studies resides fundamentally in the details, it was necessary to develop a methodology that would help us to understand and synthesise the lessons they carry and convey them to a wider policy audience. The case studies were examined from three perspectives on deployment policymaking that have taken shape over the last quarter century:

- the *Research, Development and Deployment Perspective*, which focuses on the innovation process, industry strategies and the learning that is associated with new technologies;

- the *Market Barriers Perspective*, which characterises the adoption of a new technology as a market process, focuses on decisions made by investors and consumers, and applies the analytical tools of the economist;

- the *Market Transformation Perspective*, which considers the distribution chain from producer to user, focuses on the role of the actors in this chain in developing markets for new energy technologies, and applies the tools of the management sciences.

In part the three perspectives are different vocabularies for discussing the same phenomena. Yet they are complementary – each adds something that the others lack. The strength of the R&D+Deployment perspective is its vision of the future. It focuses on the technology itself, its costs and performance, and the process of market entry through niche markets. Through the application of economic analysis, the market barrier perspective improves our understanding of barriers that impede the application of cleaner and more efficient energy technologies and provides a disciplined approach for making decisions about policy interventions. The market transformation perspective encourages sensitivity to the practical aspects of crafting policies that take account of the complex nature of actual markets and produce the desired results.

A key message developed in this book is that policy initiatives designed to facilitate the adoption of cleaner energy technologies are unlikely to succeed unless policy designers pay attention to each of these three perspectives. It is necessary to:

☐ invest in niche markets and learning in order to improve technology cost and performance;

☐ remove or reduce barriers to market development that are based on instances of market failure;

☐ use market transformation techniques that address stakeholders' concerns in adopting new technologies and help to overcome market inertia that can unduly prolong the use of less effective technologies.

Around this central theme, a close reading of the IEA case studies revealed more detailed messages about the nature of successful policy-making. Some key points are:

■ Deployment policy and programmes are critical for the rapid development of cleaner, more sustainable energy technologies and markets. While technology and market development is driven by the private sector, government has a key role to play in sending clear signals to the market about the public good outcomes it wishes to achieve.

■ Programmes to assist in building new markets and transforming existing markets must engage stakeholders. Policy designers must understand the interests of those involved in the market concerned and there must be clear and continuous two-way communication between policy designers and all stakeholders. This calls for the assignment of adequate priorities and resources for this function by governments wishing to develop successful deployment initiatives.

- Programmes must dare to set targets that take account of learning effects; i.e., go beyond what stakeholders focused on the here-and-now may consider possible.

- The measures that make up a programme must be coherent and harmonised both among themselves and with policies for industrial development, environmental control, taxation and other areas of government activity.

- Programmes should stimulate learning investments from private sources and contain procedures for phasing out eventual government subsidies as technology improves and is picked up by the market.

- There is great potential for saving energy hidden in small-scale purchases, and therefore the gathering and focusing of purchasing power is important.

- Most consumers have little interest in energy issues *per se*, but would gladly respond to energy efficiency measures or use renewable fuels as part of a package with features they do care about.

In the end it is the combined effect of technology potential and customer acceptance that makes an impact on the market and hence on energy systems. Developing a deeper understanding of both, including how they are influenced by the actions of government, is an essential ingredient of effective deployment policy.

CHAPTER 1: IN SEARCH OF A COMPREHENSIVE APPROACH TO MARKET DEVELOPMENT POLICY

Technology and Economic Change

Technological change has become a part of normal life in modern industrial societies and this state of continuous flux is recognised as a primary source of economic growth. Markets for familiar goods and services are transformed to accommodate new ways of doing things; markets for entirely new products seem to take root overnight. In some periods of modern history a great number of small and large changes over an extended period have been instigated by a specific technological development and their collective effect has been a dramatic transformation in the way things are done. The exploitation of the railway, the automobile, jet travel and now the computer are classic examples. One can easily imagine that we are now in the early stages of another such transformation, in this case towards energy systems that will be environmentally benign and deliver long-term energy security and stability.

If that hypothesis holds, this next episode of dramatic change will be distinguished by some new features. The big changes of the 19th and 20th centuries were driven by the promise of dazzling new opportunities. In contrast, the transformation of our energy systems is now being driven by the need to avoid the negative side-effects of economic activity. While the beginnings of change came in the 1970s and were motivated by the threat that energy scarcity would interfere with our high standard of living, the motivation for change is now dominated by concern for the environment.

That difference presents a new kind of challenge. Governments played important roles in all of the earlier dramatic changes in our economies referred to above, including an important involvement in the processes of research, development and the deployment of new technologies. But in those situations, once the promise of the new technologies became evident, it was not necessary for governments to motivate a reluctant private sector into getting involved. This time it is and this challenge will be made more difficult by the current political ethos, which favours minimal interference by governments in the operation of markets.

Fortunately, in regard to finding and implementing technological solutions to problems, there is a long history of cooperation between government and the private sector. The development and deployment of modern transportation technology, the computer, and the current communication revolution based on the internet and the wireless telephone have all been in part dependent on government policy and on cooperation between R&D entities in the public and private sectors. Likewise the energy system can be transformed through a continuation of that spirit of cooperation. The private sector is empowered with the know-how and capacity for innovation needed to deliver the results; governments bear the responsibility to express the collective will in regard to the need for change and to convey it in the form of effective policies.

In such a world the question of how governments design and manage their energy policies is fundamental. This book is about one aspect of the much larger challenge discussed above: how to approach the design and implementation of government policies to facilitate the development of markets for the energy technologies that will be the building blocks of a transformed energy system.

Understanding Market Development Policy

In this sort of policy environment it is more important than ever for governments to recognise the part they must play in getting better energy technologies into the marketplace competently and with a light touch. Policy-makers must understand the markets concerned and they must have a highly developed capacity to mount effective programmes. In regard to both objectives, experience is the best teacher.

In fact, a large body of this kind of experience has been built up in IEA countries over the last quarter century. Since the energy crises of the 1970s governments have been active, to varying degrees, in running programmes to encourage the development and adoption of cleaner and more efficient energy technologies. There is much to be gained by reflecting on what can be learned from such experience. To this end, the IEA invited Member countries to prepare case studies on successful market development policies so that national experience could be shared. Government officials in 10 IEA countries responded to the invitation with a total of 20 case studies; the European Commission and an international cooperative research programme each provided an additional study. The whole set of 22 case studies was discussed in depth at a workshop in November 2001, entitled *Technologies Require Markets: Best Practices and Lessons Learned in Energy Technology Deployment Policies*. Analysis of the case studies by IEA staff members and independent consultants, as well as the open discussion of workshop participants, form the basis of this book.[1]

Information exchanges of this sort clearly benefit those who participate in them. It is always stimulating for policy practitioners to see how other people in other situations are coping with the range of problems that have been occupying them. However, attempting an overall analysis that is transferable across countries is a much larger challenge.

A case study describes a single instance of a broader phenomenon. If it is well done, it can enhance our understanding of it by helping us to think about it in detail and take account of what actually happens when ideas are put into practice. It can be especially rich when it has been written by people directly involved in the experience reported upon. At the same time, the picture conveyed by a case study depends

---

1. The case studies are summarised briefly in Chapter 2 and short descriptions of the results of the projects reported on are provided in an Annex at the end of this book. The CD-ROM attached to this book contains the full text of the Case Studies and Summaries of Case-Study Findings.

strongly on its context. The details of the design of a policy and its effects depend on the traditions, culture, politics and economic structure that prevail in the country where it is applied. National energy supply systems differ greatly – they are the result in each country of a long development process conditioned by natural resource endowments and institutional constraints that guide resource exploitation and technology choices. Consumer behaviour and patterns of energy demand are social and commercial constructs that depend on economic structure, tradition and cultural values. Furthermore, a case study may reflect the particular perspective of the person who has written it. For this book, the reports were typically prepared by people involved in technology deployment programme management. These are the people who are likely to have the best grasp of the overall story to be told, but they tell it from a particular vantage point, which may not adequately account for the experiences of other groups involved, such as industrial participants and the public.

To respond to the challenge of interpreting information that is so dependent on context and the vantage points of individual authors, it was necessary to apply a methodology based on two principles: extensive comparisons across case studies dealing with similar phenomena and the conscious application of an analytical framework. This analytical approach is referred to as 'triangulation', because it involves looking at the set of case studies from three different perspectives (Nilsson and Wene, 2002). The objective was to see whether this sort of analysis would lead to a more comprehensive understanding of the experiences reported on in the case studies, and one that would help to distinguish the generic and transferable lessons from the specific aspects of different national experiences.

Three Perspectives

The three perspectives used to analyse the case studies are based on three aspects of technology market development policy that can be easily discerned, though they also overlap considerably.

■ The *research, development and deployment perspective* focuses on the nature of innovation, industry strategies and the learning process associated with new technologies. At the centre of this perspective is a well-recognised phenomenon that has an important role in both technology development and policy-making. Private industry R&D stimulated by investments in a new technology, and the 'learning-by-doing' that comes with its use, improve technical performance and reduce cost. Governments can play a valuable role in this process with policies and programmes that support initial deployment of new technologies. That insight, combined with the mind set of people involved in R&D and technology deployment, gives this perspective an orientation towards the future, one in which learning and adaptation to better technologies are a normal part of the process of societal change.

■ The *market barriers perspective* characterises the adoption of a new technology as a market process and focuses on the frameworks within which decisions are made by investors and consumers. Anything that slows the rate at which the market for a technology expands can be referred to as a market barrier. The emphasis in this perspective is on understanding such barriers and in what circumstances there might be a legitimate role for governments to play in reducing them. In this case the mind-set of the economist is evident. Economic analysis and the discipline it promotes is central to the barriers perspective.

■ The *market transformation perspective* focuses on what needs to be done in practical terms to build markets for new energy technologies. It is concerned with the behaviour and roles of market actors, how their attitudes guide decisions and how these attitudes can be influenced. It is about the craft of market development programmes and the experience of implementing them.

The strength of the research, development and deployment perspective is its vision of the future; the market transformation perspective encourages sensitivity to the practical aspects of crafting policies to get results; and the market barrier perspective leads to policies that work efficiently and generate net value. A key message developed in this book is that a combination of the three perspectives is needed to make good policy that helps to facilitate the adoption of new energy technologies.

Figure 1.1. Putting Together an Overall Perspective on Technology Market Development

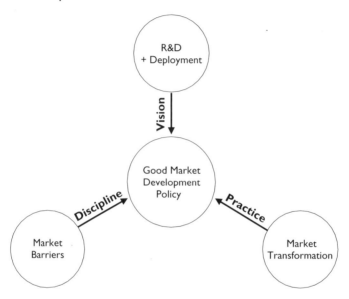

What is to Come

A brief survey of the IEA case studies is presented in Chapter 2. It indicates the range of policies and programmes covered by them and conveys an 'aerial view' of their character and the broad issues raised by them.

Chapters 3, 4 and 5 deal in turn with the three perspectives defined above. Each chapter contains a discussion of how that perspective approaches the policy aspects of facilitating the adoption of new energy technologies. It should be noted at the outset that this is not a 'How to...' book, in the sense of providing recipes for constructing policies consistent with each perspective. That would be a much larger project. It is rather intended to convey the essential ideas of each approach, illustrate them with reference to the case studies that are the information source for the book, and discuss the importance of applying all three sets of ideas in a comprehensive approach to the making of policy.

Chapter 6 is a discussion of some analytical tools used in market development policy and the difficulties involved in evaluating its impacts. Chapter 7 conveys the results of our attempts to understand the case studies in a framework based on a synthesis of all three policy perspectives and Chapter 8 presents our conclusions in summary form.

CHAPTER 2: AN OVERVIEW OF THE CASE STUDIES

Actions by government in support of market development for new energy technologies come in many shapes and sizes. Some are big, some small. Some focus on very specific technologies, some are concerned with a broad range. An action might be directed to a narrow market niche, an industry, a collection of markets that make up a broad sector of the economy, or even to all energy users. Some policy measures focus on final consumers; some of them target decision makers in service industries and some are directed to suppliers of technology. The case studies collected for this work cover all of these variations and more.

The purpose of this chapter is to convey a broad sense of the policies and programmes reported on in the case studies, with he objective of setting the stage for a more analytical discussion of market development policy in the chapters that follow. We do that by way of a series of thumbnail sketches of the individual case studies. Additional material and analytical commentary on the studies is brought into Chapters 3-5 to illustrate various aspects of the three policy perspectives discussed in this book.

Most readers will simply want to browse through the short sketches set out below to get an idea of the variety of deployment measures that have proven to be successful in IEA countries. The case study reports can be consulted, however, on the attached CD-ROM in the file named 'Case Studies'. Besides the full text of the case study reports, the CD contains a file called 'Summaries of Case-Study Findings' which for each case study presents an overview of targeted technologies, policy mechanisms, relations to the three perspectives and actors involved in the deployment programme. Also included on the CD are papers presented at the '*Technologies*

Require Markets' Workshop by three rapporteurs, each of whom discussed the case studies from the vantage point of one of the three perspectives described in Chapters 3-5 (Kliman, 2001; Lund, 2001; Schrattenholzer, 2001). At various points throughout this book, material has been drawn from these three papers.

To make browsing easier the case study descriptions are organised into groups, as follows:

Collecting the Case Studies

The IEA's Committee on Energy Research and Technology got this exercise in information exchange underway by inviting its members to report on successful policy efforts in their respective countries. Short descriptions of projects were submitted, from which 22 were chosen as subjects for the case studies. The government officials who prepared the reports in each participating country worked independently, but organised their material according to a template provided by a project group set up by the IEA Secretariat. They reported under five main headings: Policy Objectives, Design and Development, Actors and Participants, Monitoring and Evaluation, and Program Results. The objective was to share their experience of making and implementing policy in a practical context. Due to the broad variation in the types of policies that could be considered, the case study template was made open and flexible rather than highly detailed and constraining. Not surprisingly the focus and the analytical depth of the stories submitted by the national authors vary considerably across the 22 reports, with differing emphases on the various possible issues that could be treated – economic, organisational, administrative, communication, management and so on.

Table 2.1 shows the countries that submitted case studies, the names of the programmes reported on and their start dates. Some programmes were started recently. Of the older ones, many continue to operate, either because they involve programmed stages that are still in progress or because they are open-ended. In many instances current versions of these programmes have been built on the experience of earlier versions.

- ■ End-use technologies ready for use;
  - • Energy Efficiency Best Practice,
  - • Technology Procurement,
  - • Other Building Sector Programmes;
- ■ Renewable Energy Technologies;
- ■ Fossil-based Technologies;
- ■ Technology Transfer.

Table 2.1: Deployment Policy Case Studies

Country	CS No.	Case Study Title	Start Year
Austria	1	The deployment of biomass district heating	80
	2	Thermoprofit: Reducing energy consumption in buildings	99
Canada	3	Renewable energy deployment initiative in space and water heating/cooling	98
Denmark	4	Labelling for small buildings to save energy and water	82
Finland	5	Diesel engines for combined-cycle power generation	95
Germany	6	Solarbau: Energy efficiency and solar energy in the commercial building sector	95
	7	Wind power for grid connection – the 250 MW wind programme	89
Japan	8	Photovoltaic power generation – from R&D to deployment	93
Netherlands	9	Deployment of high efficiency heat recovery for domestic ventilation	95
	10	Photovoltaic covenant	97
	11	Deployment of renewable energy in a liberalised energy market by fiscal instruments	96
Sweden	12	Market transformation: lighting	91
	13	Market transformation: heat pumps	93
	14	Environmentally-adapted energy systems in Baltic Sea region	92
United Kingdom	15	Energy efficiency best practice	89
United States	16	Unconventional natural gas exploration and production	78
	17	Sub-compact fluorescent lamps	98
	18	Clean coal technology demonstration	85
	19	Industrial assessment centres	76
	20	Motor challenge and BestPractices programs	92
European Union	21	Energy + refrigerator/freezer procurement	99
International	22	IEA/SolarPACES START Missions	97

End-use Technologies Ready for Use

The state of development of a technology affects the kind of policies used to build a market for it. Some market development issues need to be dealt with long before a technology is ready for mass adoption and the measures taken will vary accordingly. At the mature end of the development spectrum, one finds a range of end-use technologies that are either entirely ready for wide adoption (e.g., various forms of building insulation) or require small steps toward further development to be more widely marketable. The most obvious examples in the latter category are technologies that are well developed in a generic sense but require adaptations for particular uses or particular market segments (e.g., compact fluorescent lamps and vacuum-panel insulation for electrical appliances). Also at this end of the spectrum are cases in which systems analysis shows that well proven technologies can be applied in new ways (e.g., new ways of using electric motors).

Energy Efficiency Best Practice

Consistent with a central theme in this book – that technological change involves an ever-present learning process – information dissemination programmes have an important role in building markets for new technologies. In several countries governments have developed 'best-practice' programmes as efficient vehicles for conveying information. Typically such programmes are carried out for sponsoring governments by subsidiary agencies or private corporations, which develop specialised expertise on reaching the buyers of a wide range of energy technologies at key decision points.

The United Kingdom's **Energy Efficiency Best Practice Programme** (CS15) is a pioneer in this area. In operation since 1989 and highly developed, it is notable for being very market-oriented and having a business-style approach to management. Its focus is on saving energy in industry, buildings and the business use of transport.

The objective is straight-forward: help organisations to cut energy bills by 10-20 percent. Do it by providing the independent advice and assistance needed to persuade them to use cost-effective technologies and management techniques. While much information is conveyed in response to individual queries, the core output is a portfolio of descriptive and prescriptive publications ranging from detailed technical reports to simple leaflets. For every £1 of expenditure, the programme must provide a benefit of at least £5/year of energy savings. By 1999 the Energy Efficiency Best Practice Programme had stimulated energy savings in excess of £650 million/year, equivalent to over 4 million tonnes/year of carbon savings.

The American *BestPractices Programme* is an amalgamation of several energy efficiency activities of the Office of Industrial Technologies in the US Department of Energy. Case Study 20 focuses primarily on one component of it, the **Motor Challenge Programme**, which promotes energy efficiency in motor systems. The American programme is more decentralised than the UK approach. It centres on partnerships with key industrial trade associations, which leverage the funding provided by USDOE. Two main policy mechanisms are used: the development of information and decision-making tools; and the development of strategic partnership networks with industrial trade associations and industrial supply companies. The first category includes training programmes, which so far have been received by more than 7 000 people.

At the centre of the Motor Challenge Programme are two ideas: the harnessing of business motivations of energy end-users, manufacturers and vendors to disseminate technical information and promote energy efficiency; and the promotion of a systems approach to managing motor systems. Industrial engineers have long known that the careful matching of the elements of an industrial plant (in the case of motor systems – motors, controls, couplings and process machinery) to the work to be performed yields far more savings than upgrading just the individual components. A market assessment carried out under the programme found that over 71 percent of total potential savings came from systems-level measures, such as improving the configuration and control schemes in pump, fan and compressor systems. An independent estimate of this one component of the US BestPractices programme found that it is a cost-effective way of saving almost 25 million US$ of energy annually.

A second case study from the US on a *BestPractices* activity reports on the **Industrial Assessment Center Programme** (CS19). It focuses on education and demonstrates again how creative partnering can be used to leverage government-funded programmes. In this case the key partners are universities – the programme trains engineering students in energy efficiency for small- and medium-sized manufacturing plants. The students, led by their teachers, perform energy audits and industrial assessments, following these up with recommendations to the manufacturers involved. Essentially this is an information dissemination programme, but with an interesting potential for long-lasting and continuing effects. Young engineers are being motivated in regard to energy efficiency; and there is every reason to expect that they will continue to apply their knowledge throughout their careers. Even without this long-term effect, which would be difficult to monitor, an evaluation of the programme by the Oak Ridge National Laboratory concludes that in 1999 its energy assessments resulted in a benefit/cost ratio of 4.9 for the first year after the assessment. The true ratio will be much higher because energy savings will continue to accrue in the future.

Technology Procurement

Competitive procurement processes can be used to encourage equipment suppliers to develop and market specific types of energy technologies according to a set of specifications defined in a policy package. Suppliers are typically rewarded with assured sales. This is a useful approach when technologies are close to being ready for the market but require additional development with a particular eye on what potential buyers are looking for. At the same time, the specification list can include measures intended to establish marketing procedures suited to the equipment involved. A procurement programme is an economical tool because by engaging equipment suppliers it combines the pursuit of technical and market development objectives in one policy and it leaves most of the detailed decisions on how to achieve goals in the hands of the suppliers. An important step in launching a procurement programme is consultation with all stakeholders in the market. The needs of potential buyers have to be identified and understood in depth and the scope for supplier-response to these needs explored. The case studies indicate that this consultation stage needs to be extensive and the whole programme needs to be highly organised.

Procurement programmes in Sweden are the subjects of two case studies. Swedish efforts in this area go back to the early 1990s and became well known in policy circles. Case Study 12, entitled *Market Transformation: Lighting*, reports on a programme carried out in 1991-92 to build a market for high-frequency electronic ballasts, which can result in electricity savings of 20-25 percent. The ballasts can be marketed as part of a package of improved product characteristics that will be attractive to consumers; for instance, by combining them with new luminaire designs and effective control, they bring improved light quality and better lighting control. A buyers group was formed in Sweden and guaranteed a direct purchase of 26 000 ballasts, with an option on a further 26 000. Sales of high-frequency lighting in Sweden prior to 1992 amounted to about 5 000 units. A programme to demonstrate high-frequency lighting to potential buyers was undertaken concurrently with the procurement project. The market grew rapidly following the programme; about 60-70 percent of luminaire sales in Sweden are now of the high-frequency variety.

Case Study 13, *Market Transformation: Heat Pumps*, reports on a two-year procurement programme started near the end of 1993 to encourage the development of reliable, cheaper and improved heat pumps for detached houses. The purchaser group, which consisted of a variety of potential buyers, including some from other Nordic countries, guaranteed the purchase of at least 2 000 units of the winning models. At the time this was about the level of a year's sales of residential heat pumps in Sweden. The procurement was combined with other activities supporting the market penetration of the winning models. This included a subsidy for the first trial batch, positive labelling, education for professionals and information dissemination to suppliers and the public. New heat pumps resulting from the programme have been marketed since the end of 1995. Sales by the end of 1996 were estimated to be between 4 000-5 000 units.

An American case study on procurement, *Sub-Compact Fluorescent Lamps* (CS17), provides interesting detail on the role of stakeholder consultation. In early 1998 the US Department of Energy set out to develop the market for a new generation of smaller, brighter and less expensive CFLs – a sub-compact lamp. A multi-stage consultation was organised with representatives of the initial target market and a comprehensive list of related stake-holder groups. This included building owners and operators, housing trade associations, lighting suppliers, energy efficiency specialists and retailers. The consultation process identified several market barriers, which were then used to define a procurement programme. The key barriers to be responded to by participating manufacturers were lamp size and price, but other more subtle barriers were taken on as well.[2] The initial sales goal of one million lamps was exceeded by more than 50 percent and five manufacturers commercialised new products; as a result of the programme, 16 new lamp models have been introduced into the US market at reasonable prices. This programme departed from the usual practice of procurement programmes intended to build markets for new technologies in an interesting way, in that it did not guarantee purchases of newly-developed products in advance.

Finally, efforts are underway to use the procurement technique in an international cooperative framework, as described in Case Study 21 on the European Union's *Energy+ Refrigerator/Freezer Procurement* programme.[3] A pilot project started in 1999 has pursued increased

---

2. These are discussed in Chapter 6.
3. The EU programme is not the only attempt to use this tool in an international framework. It has also been attempted in two of the IEA's international cooperative R&D programmes – the Demand-Side Management Programme (see http://dsm.iea.org/NewDSM/Work/Tasks/3/task3.asp) and the Solar Heating and Cooling Progamme (see http://www.iea-shc.org/ and go to Task 24 under the 'Research Tasks' link).

market penetration for highly efficient refrigerator-freezers. Ten European countries were involved. This is an ambitious effort in light of the need to take account of national particularities in project design. The 10 countries are different not only in terms of climate and culture, but also in terms of the structure of markets and frameworks of governance. The Energy+ programme has therefore had to take a more fluid approach to designing procurement policies; it does not involve the tight link between product specifications and winners of a design competition that characterise the typical national procurement competition. At one level, the programme can be viewed as a focused approach to facilitating communication between end-users, policy stakeholders and appliance manufacturers. The features that consumers want can be effectively made known to manufacturers, who will be encouraged to supply new products on a larger scale. Approximately 100 organisations, representing more than 15 000 retail outlets and the management of more than one million dwellings, joined the initial project.

Other Building Sector Programmes

While several of the programmes discussed above relate to energy use in buildings, there are other programmes included in the case studies that are more specifically focused on buildings as energy-using systems. The building and construction sector presents a great challenge to the designers of technology deployment policies because it is highly fragmented. A large array of different market players influence technology and design decisions, each type working in its own accepted niche with long-established operating procedures that are subject to much inertia. In such a setting it is not effective to encourage greater energy efficiency by having a separate market development programme for each building-related technology. It is better to approach the market on its own interrelated terms, pinpoint the key decision makers in different parts of the system and find ways to encourage them to make better energy choices. Several case studies illustrate how policy designers have been effective in doing this.

Energy service companies were developed in the early stages of energy conservation programmes in part to deal with the market fragmentation problem in the building sector. In effect, a new market took form to provide information gathering and analytical services for energy users. Case Study 2, *Thermoprofit – Reducing Energy Consumption in Buildings*, describes a project to improve the dissemination and effective application of energy efficiency information, in large part by improving the performance of energy service companies. It involves the use of third party financing, energy performance contracting and quality labelling. The programme originated in the Austrian city of Graz, though it operates at a regional level and has the potential of developing multi-regional networks.

The Danish programme on *Labelling for Small Buildings to Save Energy and Water* (CS4) provides for energy audits and 'energy labels' in the housing sector. The seller of a house must have an audit performed by an approved consultant before a sale takes place. As discussed further in Chapter 4, in addition to the direct effects on the houses audited, this sort of programme helps to make energy efficiency considerations a normal part of housing market transactions. The case study reports that more than 10 percent of all single-family houses in Denmark had an energy label after the scheme was in effect for $3\frac{1}{2}$ years.

The Dutch programme to encourage the *Deployment of High Efficiency Heat Recovery for Domestic Ventilation* (CS9) involves three types of activities: improved information dissemination, improvements in equipment and the inclusion of mechanical ventilation with heat recovery in building standards. The last measure works through an energy performance standard that must be satisfied by new buildings in the Netherlands. The installation of a high-efficiency ventilation system with heat recovery is one option that can be included among the list of things that a builder does in order to satisfy the standard. Such ventilation systems were included in less than 1 percent of new houses in the Netherlands in 1995; in 1999 they were included in 10 percent of them and the upward trend was expected to continue.

Renewable Energy Technologies

Some technologies based on renewable energy sources also relate to the building sector in ways similar to the end-use technologies discussed above; others are more closely associated with developments in the electricity supply sector. A German project straddles both categories. Demonstrating that buildings could be optimised in relation to the use of solar energy was the guiding objective in Germany's *Solarbau: Energy Efficiency and Solar Energy in the Commercial Building Sector* (CS6). It consists of up to 25 demonstration projects involving non-residential buildings, geographically distributed over all regions of Germany. Started in 1995, the programme is expected to last for 10 years with a budget of approximately 5 million euros. The idea is to integrate passive and active solar design with advanced heating, ventilation and air-conditioning (HVAC) techniques and innovative thermal insulation. This will involve the development of components, planning tools and an evaluation and information program called *SolarBau: MONITOR*.

A Canadian programme, the *Renewable Energy Deployment Initiative* (CS3) is intended to stimulate demand for renewable energy systems in the heating and cooling of space and water. It consists of two policy mechanisms: financial incentives and targeted market development initiatives. The latter involves the development of partnerships with stakeholders, strategy development, market assessments and implementation activities. So far, market development strategies have been prepared for ground-source heat pumps, solar water- and air-heating systems and biomass combustion systems, all three for industrial, commercial and institutional buildings. A fourth strategy, for residential swimming pools, was in preparation when the case study was submitted.

The Japanese programme to develop photovoltaic power takes its place among the most ambitious of those covered by the IEA case studies. Case Study 8, *Photovoltaic Power Generation – from R&D to Deployment*, describes an effort that has been very large and broad-ranging in its activities, while at the same time being focused on specific targets. Its origins trace back to 1974, when Japan reacted quickly after the 1973 oil crisis to begin expanding its energy options. The current version of the programme involves an overall target, set in 1998, of having 5 000 MW of installed photovoltaic (PV) capacity by 2010. The case study notes the possibility that residential PV-systems will one day become conventional. Over 10 000 residential units have been installed annually. Approximately 200 MW were in place by the end of FY1999.

Both R&D activities and programmes more directly focused on developing markets are included in the programme. The R&D targets are guided by an understanding of the learning-by-doing process (more on this in Chapter 3) and also involve specific technology-development objectives: new technologies for the practical application of PV power generation systems; a low-energy-consumption manufacturing process for solar grade silicon; a practical technology for making high-efficiency multicrystalline silicon solar cells; and advanced manufacturing technologies for PV power generation systems. The deployment programme seeks in general to develop PV-markets and also to demonstrate the endurance of PV-systems. Activities include field tests, subsidies for residential PV use and support of new businesses involving PV power.

The market for PV power is also being developed in the Netherlands. Case Study 10 reports on the *Photovoltaic Covenant*, a voluntary programme backed up with funding for subsidies and R&D; this includes resources from the private sector. The Covenant has resulted in a network of active participants: energy distribution companies, PV manufacturers, stakeholders in the building sector, R&D institutions and government agencies. The initial Covenant was started for three years in 1997. Government funding for R&D is in the area of solar cells, components for grid-connection applications, autonomous PV systems and pilot projects in buildings. On deployment, the programme had a target of 7.7 MW of grid-connected PV in the built environment in the year 2000. That target was reached; at the time the case study was prepared discussion was underway on a target of 250 MW by 2007 for a second Covenant.

The Netherlands has also mounted a broadly-based programme in support of the ***Deployment of Renewable Energy in a Liberalised Energy Market by Fiscal Instruments*** (CS11). This programme is different from many of the others discussed here in that it operates on an economy-wide basis, backing up more focused deployment programmes, but is also capable of producing additional results independently of them. It is an important part of the Dutch government's effort to achieve its goal of having 10 percent of all energy used coming from renewable sources by 2020. The share at the time the report was prepared was 1.2 percent.

Some elements of the Dutch fiscal programme were introduced over the past decade, including a tax on the use of electricity and natural gas, voluntary agreements with players in the energy sector and industry in general (including the PV Covenant, discussed above) and various subsidies for new initiatives (e.g., tax credits, favourable interest rates and accelerated depreciation). Two important components were added in 2001. One is the availability of 'green electricity' in a fully liberalised electricity market. Consumers pay an additional tariff when they buy it, but in return are exempted from paying the energy tax; 3.5 percent of households have responded to this offer. The second is a legally-based system, as distinct from the voluntary system that preceded it, of tradable certificates in the electricity distribution industry in support of targets for energy produced from renewable sources.

German support for the development of renewable-sourced electric power has also been broad, though wind power was the main focus in the programme described in Case Study 7, ***Wind Power for Grid Connection – the 250 MW Wind Programme***. In addition to direct subsidies, electricity producers benefited under the programme from a system of compensation for the higher costs of using renewables; this was defined by the Electricity Feed Law (EFL) of 1991. This legislation has been replaced by the Renewable Energy Law (REL) of 2000, which is designed to expand the effect of the EFL to reach a broader range of renewables and also to make adjustments that respond to the current stage of liberalisation of electricity markets in Europe. The 250 MW Wind Programme was focused strongly on the demonstration of technologies to deal with technical barriers and includes an ambitious data collection activity on the technical and operating performance of wind turbines. Investment targets have been achieved at much higher levels than originally expected and a substantial equipment manufacturing industry that competes internationally has been developed due to the combined effects of the 250 MW Wind Programme and the EFL/REL. The contracting phase of the programme was completed at the end of 1995; the closing date for the whole programme is scheduled for 2006.

A long-standing renewable energy programme in Austria was motivated in part by the objective of supporting agriculture. A significant amount of the financial resources for the **Deployment of Biomass District Heating** (CS1) has come from the federal agriculture ministry. Started in 1980, more than 500 district heating plants that use wood chips, industrial wood waste or straw as fuel were established by 1999. Plants operate at levels between a few hundred kW and 10 MW; about two-thirds have power less than 1500 kW. Subsidies provided for agricultural co-operatives usually included a soft loan and a direct subsidy, with net-cash-value amounting to about 50 percent of the total investment-costs of the project. Commercial operators of district heating plants were eligible for a 30 percent subsidy from the environment ministry. Indirect financial support was available from a 50 percent reduction in the value-added tax on wood. Surveys have shown that customer support for these plants was strongly influenced by the environmental benefits involved and by a desire to support local agriculture and self-sufficiency.

Fossil-based Technologies

The case studies convey the impression that making progress on fossil fuel technologies has called for work on fundamentally new concepts.

In some respects the challenges in this area have had more to do with classic industrial R&D, rather than with developing markets for technologies that are close to being ready for the final buyer. Energy resource exploitation and conversion, rather than end-use services, are the focus of attention. Three programmes were reported on: two from the United States that provided support for a range of technologies and one narrowly-focused programme from Finland on the development of a new type of diesel engine. While all three are about R&D programmes, they illustrate that innovation is not a linear process – effective support at the R&D stage must take account of market needs to be satisfied in later stages.

Case Study 16 is on an American programme for *Unconventional Natural Gas Exploration and Production*, which was first started in 1978 when the "gloomy, almost crisis-like outlook for the future of domestic natural gas in the late 1970s set in motion a set of national-level initiatives for adding new gas supplies." The programme was a combination of support for R&D and direct price and tax incentives for exploration and drilling. This included tax credits and the deregulation of well-head prices for natural gas from selected sources during the period when gas prices were in general regulated. Production of unconventional gas responded strongly to these incentives. In 1998 it accounted for 4,500 Bcf of supply, up from 1,500 Bcf when the programme started. Proved reserves of unconventional gas are 52 Tcf, up from less than 20 Tcf. At the end of this case study the authors set out an interesting list of 'lessons learned' from USDOE's experience with R&D policy in relation to the exploiting unconventional gas.

The US *Clean Coal Technology Demonstration* programme (CS18) is a huge R&D effort based on government-industry partnerships, so far funded by more than $5.6 billion of investment shared by the federal and state governments and industrial corporations. The programme is an example of the technology procurement approach discussed above, but in this case focused more strongly at the R&D level and carried out on a much larger scale than the examples in the end-use area. Starting in 1985, it has been implemented by way of five competitive bidding solicitations. It "is a partnership in which the federal government sets performance objectives, founded on national environmental concerns, and asks industry to respond with technical solutions." Several successful technologies that went through CCT demonstrations are noted in the case study; some of these are still pre-competitive, some have had national and international sales volumes of several billion dollars. The case study illustrates how success in deployment programmes depends strongly on learning from early experiences and on the early involvement of key stakeholders, in this case major corporations in the coal and electricity sectors.

Case study 5, *Diesel Engines for Combined-cycle Power Generation*, was built around the decision of a Finnish company specialising in diesel engines for marine use to pursue the development of a diesel concept that would be suitable for electric power plants. The requirement was thus to have an engine that can compete with gas turbines as prime movers in either single-cycle or combined-cycle power plants. A major technical barrier that has had to be dealt with is the recovery of waste heat, which leaves traditional diesel engines in ways that cannot be easily recovered for the secondary generation of power. The programme is currently in the demonstration stage with a 38 MW pilot plant. For large power plants, fuel efficiencies of 55 percent and above are expected.

Technology Transfer

National experience with market development policy can be applied to transferring knowledge across economies and some IEA countries have undertaken programmes of this kind. Two of them are reported on in the case studies. Case Study 14 from Sweden, *Environmentally-Adapted Energy Systems in the Baltic Sea Region*, reports on an effort to assist the Baltic states in making their energy systems more efficient and environmentally benign. Its main focus has been on converting heat production plants to the use of biofuels, reducing heat losses in district heating systems and improving energy efficiency in buildings. In form it is an assisted-loan programme. Much attention is paid to designing projects so that the loans granted will be self-liquidating. This has meant choosing projects that will be economically beneficial but have been held back due to classic market barriers (e.g., lack of knowledge and technical expertise, insufficient sources of finance, etc.). A substantial learning experience has occurred, since the local management of many small projects often had no experience of the discipline of loan management, nor of other aspects of contracting in a market environment. While project contractors in the early stages of the programme were typically Swedish, with the experience gained from the programme, companies in the Baltic states are now becoming prime contractors.

Case Study 22, *IEA/SolarPACES START Missions*, was prepared by an IEA cooperative R&D programme, *SolarPACES*, which stands for Solar Power and Chemical Energy Systems. *START* stands for *Solar Thermal Analysis, Review and Training*. Under the programme, an international team of experts visits a host country that has favourable solar conditions with a view to identifying promising opportunities for solar thermal power generation and assisting local personnel in the exploitation of these opportunities. Activities include technology analysis, assisting in the definition of feasibility studies, the search for financing and other developmental issues. START missions carried out in Egypt, Jordan, Brazil and Mexico are described in the case study report. The first START mission, to Egypt, has contributed to tangible results. It served as an information base and a source of independent expert evaluation for Egypt's subsequent successful application to the World Bank's Global Environment Facility for support of the construction of a 130 MW hybrid thermal electricity plant.

CHAPTER 3: A RESEARCH, DEVELOPMENT AND DEPLOYMENT PERSPECTIVE

The process by which a technology is taken from the stage of exploring a new application of scientific and engineering ideas, through the development of new equipment, and on to the market is long and complex. It is cyclical rather than linear, though it is often described as if it were linear. Decisions made throughout the process influence the likelihood that a technology will be accepted in the market. In the latter stages, when a technology is being readied for the market and used in actual market settings, the two-way feedbacks between market experience and further technical development are especially important. Market prospects are the most vital stimulant of industry R&D and the deployment of technologies is a key source of information on them. Researchers and developers understand that market development and technology development go hand in hand and this explains why they are interested in deployment issues. Because it captures this organic connection, we have labelled the first of the three perspectives we discuss in this book the *research, development and deployment perspective* – the 'R&D+Deployment perspective' in short form.

The Double Effect of Market Deployment

Investment in cleaner energy technologies in competitive markets has two positive effects. First there is the direct impact on the production and use of energy, which makes the energy system more efficient and cleaner. This is typically the effect directly targeted by governments. The deployment of new technologies also leads market actors to learn how to produce and use them more cheaply and more effectively. It is the combination of the *physical effect* and the *learning effect* that creates the real impact of energy technology deployment programmes.

The case studies that provide the source material for this book illustrate these two effects and their roles as guiding principles for the design of successful deployment programmes.

The immediate physical effect may be reduced energy use for the same service, less emissions, higher comfort or reliability, and revenues for the investor. The achievement of these sorts of beneficial effects is usually the primary rationale for government-run technology deployment programmes and growth in sales and market penetration therefore become key indicators of successful deployment programmes. However, in many instances that view is too narrow; it neglects the importance of the link between deployment programmes and private sector decisions to invest in the market learning process. Decision makers in industry may judge the initial costs of market learning for a given technology to be too high and involve too much risk. Though scarce public resources are not sufficient by themselves to bring a new technology through even the early parts of that process, effective government-supported deployment programmes can play a crucial role in encouraging private investment and activating learning processes among market participants.

The rationale for this argument is depicted in Figure 3.1, which summarises how public sector and industry R&D interact to produce a 'virtuous cycle' in which government support encourages corporations to try out new technologies in genuine market settings (Watanabe, 1995 & 1999; Wene, 1999; OECD/IEA, 2000). The two vertical arrows represent the encouragement for industry R&D and production with a new technology brought about by government policies. Expanded output and sales stimulate the 'plus' cycle in the diagram: industry R&D increases further, which enhances the technology stock, which in turn further stimulates production. The production increases also stimulate the learning process and the 'minus' cycle in the diagram, resulting in reductions in the cost of production. This further stimulates sales and the cycle reinforces itself. The figure also indicates the role of experience and learning curves, which will be discussed later in this chapter. They provide a quantitative measure of market learning and the efficiency of the feed-back from market experience ("M") to production and industry R&D, which leads to cost reductions and improved technology (Wene, 1999; OECD/IEA, 2000).

Figure 3.1. Influences on the Learning System from Public Policies

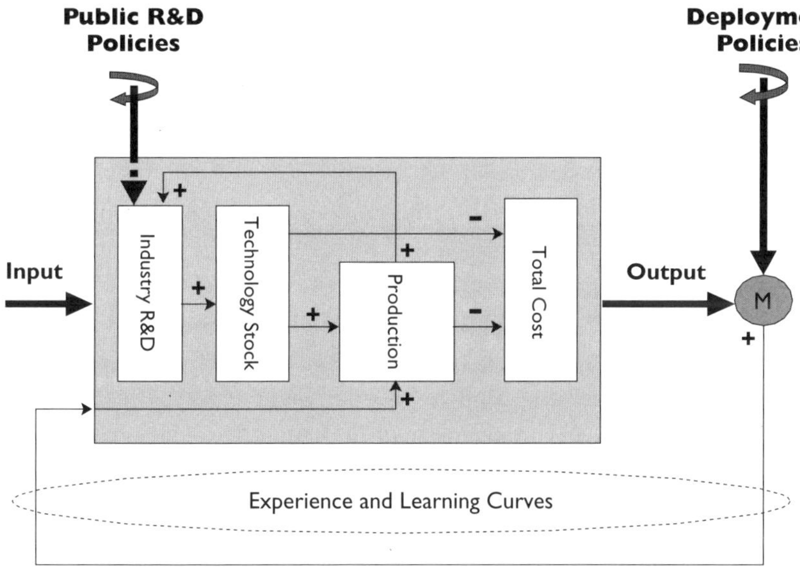

Source: OECD/IEA (2000), p. 29.

Through this process the learning effect manifests itself in succeeding generations of the technology, with associated reductions in product prices, better technical performance and improved or innovative methods of marketing and application. The technology may become attractive to additional suppliers and products produced with it will account for larger and larger segments of the market, thereby increasing the physical effects of deployment. For new technologies, improvements in cost and technical performance from one generation to the next may be substantial; in mature technologies learning usually manifests itself in better marketing and new applications of more energy-efficient and cleaner variants of the technology.

In the context of this book it is important to emphasise that while public sector R&D is important, it cannot directly bring about the cost reductions that will make the new technology competitive in the market place. "The outstanding feature of this internal learning process is that there is no virtuous cycle and no substantial cost reductions without market interactions" (OECD/IEA, 2000, p.30). Thus to provide a pay-off, the results of public R&D have to enter into the internal industry R&D process. This constitutes a powerful argument in favour of government support for technology deployment – if government is supporting research, it should also be supporting deployment.

From Public R&D to Market Learning

"I don't see how this can work." The Treasury man was sounding more than a little sceptical and was making Anna, who would lead the new programme if it got approved, apprehensive. "I agree," he continued, "that a big pilot project would improve efficiency and do a lot for getting us off the hook on CO_2 reductions. But to me the project itself looks like pie in the sky. Getting that amount of market push would take big money from the taxpayers. The subsidies would go on forever. You said yourself that this technology still doesn't compete on cost and I don't see anybody beating a path to the developer's door to buy the thing."

Anna's boss looked at the three other people around the table and stepped in – more quickly than he should have – to wind up the discussion. "Obviously the people at the lab are going to have to work more on how to get the new technology into operation. I'll suggest to my Director-General that he go to the R&D budget committee with a proposal for another stage of development work."

Anna shook her head. "No. Government R&D money has brought the technology this far but it can only do so much. At some point there has to be industry involvement. They have to get some experience from actually using the technology and they have to try out a little corner of the market. Then they'll be able to get the product design right, costs will fall, and they'll get some feel about how to approach customers when they do a large-scale launch." She looked across the table at the industry consultant. "I think you people in the industry understand how market learning reduces cost and helps to line up market players who can make the thing work. You are the people who can use a project like this one to set the stage for big market acceptance."

The industry consultant took a deep breath. He knew she was expecting him to turn the argument. How to sum up 200 years of industry experience with developing and selling new technology? Should he start with the reflections of the old clock-makers from 1866, airplane development since 1936, or maybe get more abstract and talk about the rich literature on organisational learning from the management science people? No. Not that way. Short-and-sweet is better. "Yes, it's true," he started, "market experience does reduce cost and improve performance, not only in the equipment, but also in lining up the whole distribution chain ... the wholesalers and retailers, and the service people. In fact, my company clients view such learning as a key strategic factor when they launch new products. We know that we have to price below cost for a while, but as we get experience, cost drops below price and the cash starts flowing in. And we've found that your market facilitation programmes make a big difference. Your consumer information efforts give us legitimacy with the customers; and it's great to get the product standards and energy efficiency labelling edited so that the retailers aren't afraid that they're doing something wrong. All that kind of stuff makes a big difference. Working together like that, it should be possible to phase out the subsidies right on schedule."

The man from the Treasury hesitated. Industry arguments carried weight at the Treasury. He glanced at his watch – still an hour before lunch. "OK", he said, "let's go over the highlights of the new deployment programme one more time."

Two Types of Learning

It is useful to distinguish between the different aspects of learning that a deployment programme may trigger.

Technology learning refers to the progressive reduction in costs and prices and the improvement in performance shown by all technologies as they are adopted through market processes (OECD/IEA, 2000). Most programmes that aim to reduce cost and technical barriers in the way of greater use of a technology focus on technology learning. Initial adoption of the technology in niche markets, and the prospects of larger markets in future, stimulate additional R&D by industry. At the same time, learning-by-doing and scale economies as more output is produced lead to product refinement, lower costs and larger market opportunities. Subsidies to increase market volume stimulate technology learning and technology procurement programmes, labelling and standards may also target technology learning.

There are also other types of barriers that may hinder market expansion for those technologies that are already technically mature and cost-efficient – barriers related to information flows, standards, transaction costs, financing and the organisation of markets (OECD/IEA, 1997a and 1997b). *Institutional* or *organisational learning* refers to an increase in an organisation's capability for effective action (Espejo *et al*, 1996). Applying that idea in this context, market deployment leads to organisational learning for the company developing and promoting a technology, as it learns how to overcome those barriers that are not directly related to the cost or performance of the technology itself. At the same time, the other market players (consumers, intermediaries, governments) also have the opportunity for organisational learning, but in this case the organisation being referred to is the market itself. As a new technology is deployed, the potential returns from a technology and the need to adapt to its characteristics can lead to changes in the behaviour of market actors, which in turn can affect market outcomes and the structure of markets. Examples of policies and programmes that may stimulate this type of learning are information dissemination, labelling schemes and governmental actions that bring about changes in the organisation of markets for new technologies or services related to them.

The 22 case studies deal with a broad spectrum of technologies, organisations and policies. All of them point to the importance of learning processes. How deployment programmes can stimulate and improve organisational and technology learning in efficient ways is therefore a major theme in this book. We turn our attention now to the issues and challenges involved in doing that.

Creating Conditions for Organisational Learning

The reform of energy supply systems currently underway in many IEA countries and the increasing importance of new customer supply technologies demonstrate the necessity of organisational learning in the energy system.

Historically, increasing demands for energy in industrial societies have been satisfied by the development and growth of centralised energy supply systems. Over the last century, this system learned to evolve and adapt to major shifts in the fossil fuel structure, new technologies for extracting coal, oil and gas, and new centralised technologies for generating electricity (such as nuclear reactors and natural gas combined cycle turbines). Deployment programmes in these supply-side areas have typically targeted technology learning, leaving the responsibility for organisational learning to the market actors. However, the restructuring of energy supply markets on competition policy grounds has challenged the traditional division between the supply system and its customers. In addition, it has been driven by technology developments, such as modular technologies for electricity production. For instance, micro-turbines, fuel cells, photovoltaic systems and other renewable technologies can be installed and owned by the traditional customers of electricity systems; this supports a trend towards decentralised power production. This is imposing new learning demands on both energy suppliers and their customers, as can be witnessed, for example, in the ongoing upheaval in the electricity markets of many IEA countries.

The case studies include classic examples of supply-side programmes focused on technology learning; e.g., CS16 on the exploitation of unconventional gas and CS18 on the demonstration of clean coal technologies, both from the United States. The Finnish study on diesel engines for combined cycle power generation (CS5) reflects the traditional emphasis on technology learning, but also points to the increasing involvement of energy users. Overall, however, there is a striking indication in the case studies of the new importance given to organisational learning. More than two-thirds of them deal with markets for end-use energy technologies or for decentralised energy production. All of these studies address organisational learning, though some more explicitly than others. Examples that treat organisational learning issues in direct discussion are the Austrian studies on Biomass District Heating (CS1) and the Thermoprofit programme (CS2), the Danish labelling scheme for buildings (CS4), the PV Covenant in The Netherlands (CS9), the Swedish effort to transform the heat pump market (CS13), the United Kingdom's Best Practices Programme (CS15) and the American programme of Industrial Assessment Centers (CS19).

Thus a first broad inference from the case studies is that governments in IEA countries appear to recognise, at least implicitly, the need to focus on organisational learning in deployment policies. This can be understood in light of the potential for improved energy efficiency through the use of new end-use technologies (many of which are well developed and ready for widespread use), the promise of modular and decentralised supply technologies and the widespread interest in regulatory reform. Transforming energy systems and markets to facilitate these changes may require major changes in the way market actors do their business, changes in the relations among them, and in some cases the emergence of new types of actors. Technology learning remains important because sustainable markets for new technologies ultimately depend on cost reductions. But issues such as the need for information dissemination, market restructuring and changes in consumer behaviour – which are hugely complex – are also important and they call for a new emphasis on organisational learning.

Some case studies illustrate policy tools that can stimulate technology and organisational learning simultaneously. Technology procurement programmes provide excellent examples of this possibility (as illustrated by Case Studies 12, 13, 17 and 21) because they bring together technology developers, customers and intermediaries in the chain of supply. This provides for 'concentrated learning' by all parties – producers use the customer feedback to tailor and refine the product; customers learn how the product can create value and opportunities for them; and intermediaries learn about both the product's advantages and the customer's needs, and therefore how to market and support the technology effectively.

Two additional observations relevant to organisational learning emerge from the case studies. The first observation refers to *stakeholders*. The roles of all of the stakeholders in a technology market development programme must first be analysed and understood. Representatives of relevant groups generally need to be actively engaged in the programme, in some cases even in the design phase. As a programme evolves, relations to other stakeholders may be revealed and these new stakeholders should then be brought into the programme. The Austrian Biomass-District Heating (CS1) and the Danish Labelling Scheme for Buildings (CS4) provide clear illustrations of how the success of a programme depends on stakeholder identification and engagement. They also illustrate the need to revise programmes as new organisational issues emerge.

The second observation refers to the need for *relearning*. Involving the end user in the technology deployment and development process and changing the traditional boundaries between supply and demand require major changes, not just in routines and procedures familiar to market actors, but also in the models and concepts that underpin decisions. Basic ideas on 'How we do business around here' may have to be re-evaluated, for example in the shift from centralised to decentralised power generation. Where a cleaner energy technology brings with it these sorts of 'paradigm shifts', changes in other policy domains may be necessary, notably taxes, labelling, product standards and, in the case of distributed generation, electricity market rules. However, the case studies also indicate that it is not sufficient only to change these broader policy settings; more directly targeted measures may also be necessary, such as targeted information programmes, employee training and focused technology procurement programmes.[4]

Relearning usually requires changing some fundamental processes. The literature on organisational learning makes the distinction between *single- and double-loop learning*, as depicted in Figure 3.2 below. Single-loop learning focuses on 'How to do things better'. For instance, it could involve observing the effect of putting a product on the market and then correcting production processes and routines in order to fulfil business goals. However, in a learning organisation, sensitivity to new phenomena in the market will activate a second learning loop in which the organisation's goals and the way it does business are questioned. Instead of asking 'How to do things right?' they will ask 'How to do the right things?'. Relearning is part of a double-loop process because the activities in the second loop must build on what is observed through the first loop.[5]

Relearning in this double-loop sense highlights two issues involved in deployment programmes. First, a successful deployment programme is likely to have the effect of stimulating relearning, since the product itself is likely to evolve in response to feedback from the market. Such relearning cannot be taken for granted, however, and may need to be facilitated by the deployment programme. For instance, using the scheme in Figure 3.2, a procurement programme could directly

---

4. CS1 and CS4 can again be invoked as examples of targeted measures, as can the procurement case studies: 12, 13, 17 and 22.

5. See Espejo *et al* (1996) and Morgan (1986). The latter finds that an efficient first learning loop may actually hinder relearning: "... it is interesting to note that highly sophisticated single-loop learning systems may actually serve to keep the organization on the wrong course, since people are unable or not prepared to challenge underlying assumptions." (p. 90)

influence the 'Deploy' activity[6] (by providing a market pull). Changes in standards and labelling requirements could affect the 'Observe' activity[7] (by influencing the choices of customers), and fiscal measures could affect the 'Correct' activity[8] (by influencing financing decisions and profitability thresholds). The challenge for the programme designer is to find the mix of policies and measures that prompts the enterprise and the market to reconsider their habitual ways of doing business, in order that the benefits of the new technology can be expressed and valued.

Figure 3.2. Double-loop Learning – An Adaptation and Modification of a Model in Morgan (1986)

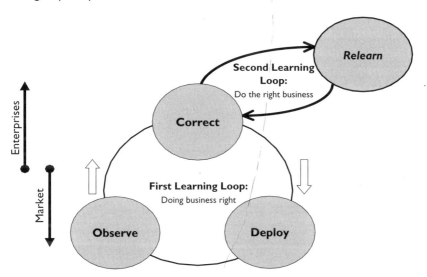

---

6. The procurement programmes in Case Studies 12, 13, 17 and 22 focus on the market deployment activity. The Motor Challenge and BestPractices programme, CS20, also focuses on the 'Deploy' activity and explicitly recognises "the challenge of changing ingrained business and engineering practices among end-users and vendors without the use of grants, rebates or other direct financial incentives."

7. One of the speakers from industry at the *'Technologies Require Markets'* workshop provided an illustration of how a company's awareness of change that will come about as a result of a deployment programme prompted relearning. The European Union's labelling scheme for cold appliances made the leading firm in that industry change its business strategy. It stranded investments on a product about to be launched in order to free up resources to develop a new product with a higher efficiency. This product was launched one year later.

8. E.g., as in the Dutch programme for renewable energy in CS11.

The second issue highlighted is that several different market actors may have to go through a process of relearning in order for the new technology to be fully accepted. For instance, changes may have to occur in a multi-stage distribution chain or new relations may have to be developed between independent entities that interact through the market.[9]

The need not only to stimulate, but also to align the relearning process among different organisations, presents a great challenge for the designers of a deployment programme. Obviously it is desirable to rely where feasible on the ability for self-organisation inherent in a well functioning market. This can occur in a situation in which market conditions favour a desired transformation and the deployment programme is needed only to act as a catalyst. Where aligning the relearning process is necessary, interaction with and among existing or would-be market actors has to be a part of the deployment programme. Such interactions can take many forms. The programme may use or foster 'champions' among market actors, who could then act as agents of change.[10] It may help to develop new frameworks for communication between stakeholders, either through direct contact or by way of market devices (e.g., competitive bidding for a guaranteed sale).[11]

The framework for thinking about organisational learning comes from the literature on management science. Though the ideas can appear rather abstract at a general level, the organisational learning concept can have a practical impact because it draws attention to the need for management systems that are open to change and the need for entrepreneurs and policy-makers to view innovation as a continuing process. Of course, the practical details ultimately have to be faced if deployment programmes are to encourage organisational learning. This requires attention to the details of how markets operate and how buyers make decisions. These kinds of issues are discussed further in the chapters on market barriers and market transformation. In

---

9. E.g., CS12 and CS13 stress the importance of involving retailers, installation and maintenance firms.

10. Case studies 1, 6 and 19 provide examples of such strategies.

11. CS10 provides an example of the establishment of a new forum for market actors. CS13 involves competitive bidding.

combination with those two perspectives, the organisational learning model contributes to the effective design of deployment policy.

Providing Opportunities for Technology Learning

There is overwhelming empirical evidence that deploying new technologies in competitive markets leads to *technology learning*, in which the cost of using a new technology falls and its technical performance improves as sales and operational experience accumulate. Experience and learning curves, which summarise the paths of falling technology costs and improving technical performance respectively, provide a robust and simple tool for analysing technology learning.[12] Viewed from the R&D+Deployment perspective, the curves provide a method to set targets and monitor programmes; this includes a way of estimating programme costs and providing a guide to phasing out programmes as technologies mature and no longer require the support of deployment measures (OECD/IEA, 2000, pp. 45-74).

The shape of the curves indicates that improvements follow a simple power law. This implies that relative improvements in price and technical performance remain the same over each doubling of cumulative sales or operational experience. As an example, Figure 3.3 shows that the prices of photovoltaic modules declined by about 20 percent as each doubling of sales occurred during the period between 1968 and 1998 (Harmon, 2001). Thus the *learning rate* for PV-modules on the world market is 20 percent.[13]

The case studies provide several examples of how deployment programmes have led to technology learning. During Japan's

---

12. For more detailed discussions, see Boston Consulting Group (1968); Abell and Hammond, (1979); and OECD/IEA (2000).

13 The experience curve is described by the following expression:
Price at year $t = P_0 * X^{-E}$,
where P_0 is a constant and X is cumulative sales. E is a (positive) experience parameter and the learning rate $= (1 - 2^{-E}) * 100$. Experience curves refer to prices; learning curves refer to technical performance.

programme for residential PV-systems, costs have been reduced from 30 US$/Wp to 7 US$/Wp;[14] in the case of wind turbines in Germany costs have been reduced by 50 percent.[15] Prices of electronic ballasts were reduced by 30 percent during the Swedish market transformation programme on lighting.[16] The observed learning rates are consistent with measurements from other sources, indicating 18-20 percent for PV-systems, but more modest values of 4-12 percent for wind turbines (Neij, 1999, Durstewitz and Hoppe-Kilpper, 1999) and ballasts (Iwafune, 2000). The tripling of markets for heat pumps in Sweden (CS13) also indicates technology learning, but data are insufficient to draw conclusions about the learning rate (Schrattenholzer, 2001).

The evidence from experience curves draws attention to the need to provide *learning opportunities* for new technologies in markets for energy services. That typically means that a supplier of energy services will have to incur costs that are greater than those incurred when incumbent technologies are used. Figure 3.4 illustrates the point with the experience curve for photovoltaic modules. For photovolvaic systems to compete against currently used technologies in central power stations, the cost of modules has to be brought down to 0.5 US$/W$_p$, indicated by the horizontal line marked 'Price competition with incumbent technology' in the diagram. The experience curve represents the price necessary for a producer of PV modules to cover the cost of production; however, in markets dominated by the incumbent technologies the producer will not obtain this price. Thus the shaded triangle represents the extra cost, *learning investments*, that will have to be covered from other sources if the market for PV-electricity is to expand and the cost of production with PV is to fall to the level of the current market price – the break-even point in the diagram.

Figure 3.4 indicates that a very large amount of learning investment will be needed to bring this technology to the break-even point based

---

14. CS8. See also OECD/IEA(2000), pp. 64-74.
15. CS7. See also OECD/IEA (2000), pp. 52-64.
16. CS12. See also Schrattenholzer (2001).

Figure 3.3. Thirty Years of Technology Learning

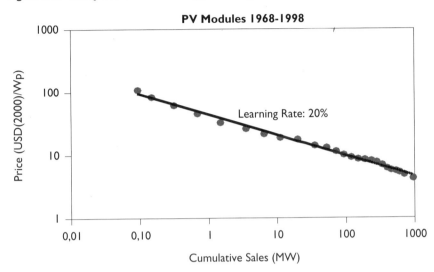

Source: Adapted from Harmon (2001).

Figure 3.4. Making Photovoltaics Break Even

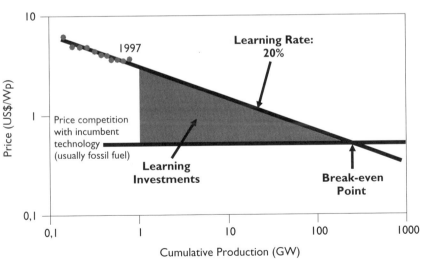

Source: OECD/IEA(2000).

on the fossil fuel technologies presently used to produce electricity from central power stations.[17] Estimates range between 50 to 100 billion US dollars. At current growth rates, 25 years of investment in learning will be required to reach the break-even point.

While some other technologies can be pushed to the break-even point for less than the amount needed for PV, it is clear that large sums of money are needed to finance learning investments. Will they come from investors in the private sector or government? The answer is both. The important point here is to be aware of the issues involved in efforts by government to activate private funding of learning investments and shorten the time horizon within which a technology will be considered a commercial endeavour. In the following section we will discuss how niche markets attract private investors and provide stepping stones to large-volume commercial markets, but first it is useful to consider some general implications of technology learning for the relations between deployment activities in the public and private sectors.

As a matter of course, the private sector finances investment in some new technologies that have not yet reached the break-even point (for example, through venture capital). This can be understood in the terms of Figure 3.4 by recognising the implications of the experience curve continuing to the right of the break-even point. The expectation is that the cost of using a new technology will fall below the current market price. Since incumbent technologies may still account for the larger market share, they will determine the market price for the energy service produced and the new technology will begin earning net profit

---

17. Figure 3.4 can be used to provide a more precise definition of learning investments for the case of an emerging new electric technology without fuel cost, such as PV. The specific learning investment, LI, per kW of capacity is

LI = P(new) − [8760*r*p(market) − O&M]/annuity,

P(new) is the price per kW for the emerging new technology at the time of investment and p(market) is the price per kWh of electricity from the currently cost-efficient (fossil fuel) technology. r is the load factor and O&M are the operation and maintenance costs at the break-even point for power plants with the new technology. The second term is the break-even price. More detailed calculations of learning investments therefore require databases with time series not only of technology prices and installations, but also of market prices and interest rates. Compare the assumption of a constant break-even price made in the figure with the curve for fossil fuel technologies in OECD/IEA(2000), Fig. 1.5, p. 21. (See also the following footnote.)

that recovers the learning investments.[18] However, existing firms tend to prefer incumbent technologies. Even if they are aware of opportunities for technology learning, they will often be cautious about investing in them and possibly for good reasons from their viewpoint. They may view the learning rate and the associated time path of learning benefits as too uncertain; and any given company may face the risk that some or all of the benefits of its learning investments can end up being captured by its competitors. Thus, if they make learning investments independently at all, they are likely to choose technologies that have already progressed substantially down the learning curve (though exceptions to this are plausible, such as in cases where new technologies have been developed through in-house R&D).

Government deployment programmes that provide assistance or incentives for private investment can thus make a crucial difference for major new technologies in the energy sector. Furthermore, the tendency towards inertia on the part of market actors creates a classic case for action from government – an instance of what economists refer to as positive externalities. If private investors are not forthcoming to undertake learning investments in a technology that is judged to be market-ready, society will benefit if government (which may have a different risk profile and lower costs of capital) puts resources into encouraging and facilitating the investment in technology learning. For practical reasons governments are not in the habit of responding to this argument for just any technology, but in the case of new energy technologies that help to achieve the governmental goals of improving energy security and reducing greenhouse gas emissions, the case for action becomes very strong.

---

18. This point is made more complex when one recognises that incumbent technologies may still be benefiting from market learning. That is, the price line for the incumbent technology should perhaps be sloping downward; it has been made a horizontal line in Figure 3.4 merely for the sake of simplicity. However, accounting for this point does not change the general thrust of the argument. Some important incumbent technologies are old enough to make the assumption of a zero-learning effect reasonable. Where this is not the case there is still no problem with the argument because the logic of the experience curve implies that added sales reduce cost faster for the new technologies than for the old ones. Consider for instance two technologies with the same learning rates of 20%, but with cumulative sales of 100 MW and 100 GW respectively. For 20% reduction in price, the first technology requires 100 MW added sales, but the second requires 100 GW.

This argument of course raises complex questions about 'picking winners' and about how much cost governments should incur when it is not clear how large the future benefits will be and to whom they will accrue. This is a large subject and an exploration of it is beyond the scope of this book. As already noted, the case study project was focused on the design and implementation of successful deployment programmes and was not intended to cover the process leading to decisions to establish programmes in the first place. However, it is worth noting here that empirically-observed learning effects are helpful when benefit-cost analysis is used to establish whether there is a rationale for a specific deployment programme. Some benefit-cost analyses neglect dynamic effects of this sort, in which case these analyses will be biased towards locking in existing technologies and their variants.[19] As well, changes in a technology and organisational learning effects can bring about changes in the nature of an energy service, which means that price and cost observations for the new form of the service may not be directly comparable to prices and costs of the old form of the service. This can lead to inaccurate conclusions about the relative efficiencies of new and old technologies and could affect benefit-cost calculations.[20] Qualitative changes of this sort are also of interest because they can provide the basis for 'niche markets', as discussed in the next section.

Strategic Niche Market Management

Specific characteristics of new technologies can add value that makes potential buyers with special needs ready to pay extra for energy services produced with them instead of with incumbent technologies. Examples of characteristics that may provide the basis for a niche market are low emissions, modularity and compatibility of a new power

---

19. See OECD/IEA (2000) pp. 84-91 for a discussion on how technology learning may create alternative technology paths.
20. The role of benefit-cost analysis is discussed further in the next chapter.

source with electricity load patterns on the grid. The niche markets may be small relative to the total potential for a technology, but they can be important from the viewpoint of providing learning opportunities. Making use of them in deployment programmes can help both to shorten the time before a new technology will be viewed as a viable commercial endeavour and provide a source of business funding for learning investments. Market leaders often use a niche market in developing a 'challenger' to an existing technology, viewing it as a stepping stone towards a mass market.

Figure 3.5 illustrates how a niche market can lead to earlier commercialisation of a technology and that the bill for learning investments can be split between public and private sources. Consider the following scenario. In the situation marked by 'A', the cost of the challenger-technology is still higher than the willingness to pay in the niche market. A subsidy can provide the difference between the actual cost and the price in the niche market. As demand at the upper end of the niche market is satisfied, the price on the niche market is reduced, but learning has also reduced the cost of providing the product. In situation 'B', cost is below the willingness-to-pay in the niche market and no public money is needed to finance learning investments, though it may still be necessary to assist with indirect support (e.g., labelling schemes and other information devices). In situations 'C' and 'D', the market leader may be in the enviable position of being able both to brand his products for a niche market that is very profitable (C) and to let one of his lesser brands feature a low-price version of the product that competes with the incumbent technology (D).

Creating and exploiting niche markets is an efficient strategy for a deployment programme, both to provide learning investments from private sources and to stimulate organisational learning among market actors. The 'Los Angeles initiative' to promote electric vehicles is viewed as a good example of strategic niche market management (Kemp, 1997). Labelling schemes can create niche markets which can be used by brand names to provide learning investments from the consumer in order to develop their new products.[21] The case studies contain several examples of how niche markets are used to set in motion interactive learning processes and technology development. For instance, organisational learning by way of niche markets is discussed in CS1 on the Austrian programme for biomass in district heating and in CS3 on the Canadian Renewable Energy Development Initiative. Japan's programme on Photovoltaic Power Generation (CS8) provides an excellent example of how niche markets are used to share learning investments between public and private sources.[22] The Dutch PV programme (CS10) shows how niche markets can be systematically used to aid technology learning.[23]

Figure 3.5: Interplay Between Niche Markets and the Experience Curve for a Technology Challenging the Incumbent Technology in the Market

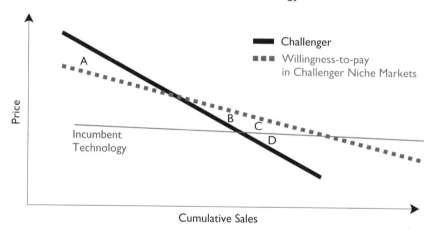

Currently one can find large potentials for energy efficiency improvements hidden in situations in which energy use appears unimportant to the

---

21. For instance, the European Union labelling scheme for cold appliances created a niche market for highly energy-efficient refrigerators. This market was exploited by the market leader (see also footnote 7). As a result, technology learning has made this originally very expensive technology available on the mass market.

22. See also Chapter 6, Figure 6.2 and OECD/IEA (2000), pp. 64-74.

23. Niche markets are discussed further in Chapter 5 and in the papers presented by the three Rapporteurs to the 'Technologies Require Markets' Workshop.

individual decision maker, though it aggregates into a large amount of energy used by all consumers taken together (e.g., energy used for standby power in computers and other electronic appliances). From the energy technology perspective, the mass markets in such cases appear highly fragmented and the need for joint relearning among market actors is correspondingly large. The strong need for organisational learning and experimentation favours a niche market approach for deployment programmes in such instances. A good example is lighting, where energy savings come in very small packages which have to be bundled together to make a difference from a policy viewpoint. The two case studies on lighting, CS12 and CS17, indicate the need to start in small niches and ensure feedback for learning both to market actors and to the deployment programmes involved.

CHAPTER 4: A MARKET BARRIERS PERSPECTIVE

Introduction

To say that something should be done to encourage the adoption of new energy technologies is the same as saying that markets for them should be developed and encouraged to grow. When radically new technologies are involved, this will require developing market infrastructure and networks from the ground up. In other cases, involving less radical change through adaptation and improvement of existing technologies and system reorganisation, the transformation of well-established existing markets may be required. Similarly markets for energy services have to be transformed to account for changes in the character of services due to the use of new technologies. In regard to both the technologies themselves and the energy services produced with them, a wide spectrum of market types is involved. For example, regarding size, markets might be small in terms of the numbers of buyers and sellers (e.g., markets for new electricity generation technologies), though very large in terms of the amount of spending that flows through them. Or they might be enormous in terms of the numbers of buyers involved because a small new technology is sold directly to final consumers (e.g., markets for energy-efficient light bulbs).

Inertia is likely to be found in well-established markets based on conventional energy technologies that have been around for many decades. For a variety of reasons – such as ingrained consumer attitudes combined with the large expense involved in trying to change them or the advantages that existing sellers have if their technologies are based on costly capital infrastructure that has been paid for in the past – the market system may be sluggish when it comes to welcoming new products. In the 1980s and 90s, many proponents of energy conservation and diversification believed that normal market processes were far too slow at bringing about the widespread use of new energy technologies that were urgently needed to enhance energy security and the environment. They suggested that this was due to various barriers in the way of the rapid market penetration of technologies that were obviously superior in their view and they advocated government action to reduce or eliminate them. Some economists responded to these arguments and a debate ensued. The economists did not dispute the existence of obstacles in the way of new technologies, but did disagree with the advocates of government action over the appropriate role of government in mitigating the barriers.[24]

Out of this debate came what we are calling the market barriers perspective, a view that focuses on the desirability of facilitating the adoption of cleaner and more efficient energy technologies, but by way of policies consistent with the underlying objectives and constraints of a market system. The objective of promoting energy conservation is still there, but subject to the constraint that the policy measures used to pursue that goal are economically efficient.[25] Put another way, it is the perspective that results when the barriers that tend to slow the rate of adoption of new technologies are identified and subjected to analysis within the framework of neoclassical economics.[26]

Market Barriers and Economic Analysis

The various market barriers that are viewed as important are by this time well known. Table 4.1 provides a summary list, along with some typical measures that are taken to alleviate the barriers. Note that a

---

24. See, for example, Sutherland (1991).

25. Economic efficiency is a rigorously defined concept that is the theoretical basis of most prescriptions offered by economists in regard to market-related issues. In a typical formal definition, an allocation of resources is said to be efficient if any reallocation would either leave everyone in the economy equally well off or would make someone worse off. The usefulness of such a definition resides in the way it throws light on situations in which resource allocation is *inefficient* and on the market conditions that are likely to be efficient, or inefficient as the case may be. How these ideas are worked out in detail can be found in any standard textbook on microeconomic theory or the theory of welfare economics.

26. Some portions of this chapter are taken from Kliman (2001), a paper on the market barriers perspective prepared for the *"Technologies Require Markets"* Workshop.

Table 4.1. Types of Market Barriers and Measures that can Alleviate them

Barrier	Key Characteristics	Typical Measures
Uncompetitive market price	Scale economies and learning benefits have not yet been realised	• Learning investments • Additional technical development
Price distortion	Costs associated with incumbent technologies may not be included in their prices; incumbent technologies may be subsidised	• Regulation to internalise 'externalities' or remove subsidies • Special offsetting taxes or levies • Removal of subsidies
Information	Availability and nature of a product must be understood at the time of investment	• Standardisation • Labelling • Reliable independent information sources • Convenient & transparent calculation methods for decision making
Transactions costs	Costs of administering a decision to purchase and use equipment (overlaps with "Information" above)	
Buyer's risk	• Perception of risk may differ from actual risk (e.g., 'pay-back gap') • Difficulty in forecasting over an appropriate time period	• Demonstration • Routines to make life-cycle cost calculations easy
Finance	• Initial cost may be high threshold • Imperfections in market access to funds	• Third party financing options • Special funding • Adjust financial structure
Inefficient market organisation in relation to new technologies	• Incentives inappropriately split – owner/designer/user not the same. • Traditional business boundaries may be inappropriate • Established companies may have market power to guard their positions	• Restructure markets • Market liberalisation could force market participants to find new solutions
Excessive/ inefficient regulation	Regulation based on industry tradition laid down in standards and codes not in pace with development	• Regulatory reform • Performance based regulation
Capital Stock Turnover Rates	Sunk costs, tax rules that require long depreciation & inertia	• Adjust tax rules • Capital subsidies
Technology-specific barriers	Often related to existing infrastructures in regard to hardware and the institutional skill to handle it	• Focus on system aspects in use of technology • Connect measures to other important business issues (productivity, environment)

Source: IEA (1997a).

list of this sort is not comprehensive and is not meant to suggest that the individual barriers are tight categories. The barriers overlap and there is interaction between them and their effects on decisions to invest in new technologies.[27]

According to the principles of market economics, government should intervene in the economy only in a situation in which the market fails to allocate resources efficiently and where the intervention will improve net social welfare. In the 'strong' form of this view, barriers in the way of the adoption of new technologies should be dealt with by government action only if they involve *market failure*. In those cases, government should intervene to correct the market failure (again, subject to the intervention increasing net social welfare). Once this has been done, according to the market barriers perspective, government should leave decisions on the purchase of new technologies to the private sector.

Thus one has to consider to what extent the barriers identified involve market failure and whether there are any qualifications to the market failure argument. There are three levels to this consideration.

Market Failure in Relation to Typical Market Barriers

Some of the market barriers shown in Table 4.1 – such as the cost of collecting information and administering market transactions, the risk of product failure, the high cost of finance for small borrowers, and others included in the table – are normal and inherent aspects of the operation of most markets and they should be allowed to influence decisions in energy markets just as they influence decisions in all other markets. That is, these barriers do not usually satisfy the market failure criterion because they involve necessary costs that have to be covered for all goods and services; the existence of the barriers themselves does not provide a reason for favouring new energy technologies, which

---

27. A fuller discussion than is possible here is necessary to understand them in depth. See, for instance, Hirst & Brown (1990), OECD/IEA (1997a), Ch. 1, and Reddy (1991).

should have to compete for investment dollars with everything else of value if resources are to be allocated efficiently. However, that is only a first step in making a judgement. Blanket judgements on these matters are inadequate because in specific markets these barriers may have characteristics that do cause market failure. A better understanding of the nature of market failure is necessary to explore this argument. While a thorough primer on the subject is not possible here, it is useful to sketch the general lines of argument.

Most instances of market failure involve *externalities,* which occur in a market transaction if any of the costs or benefits involved in it are not accounted for in the price paid for the product that is exchanged. If there are costs that are external to the market (i.e., the buyer does not pay some of the costs incurred in producing the product), a negative externality occurs. If there are external benefits, a positive externality occurs.

An example of a classic market barrier that can involve market failure is the cost and inconvenience to consumers of finding and analysing information about energy-saving equipment. Consumers require small amounts of technical knowledge to become aware that a useful new energy-efficient product is available and to evaluate the claims of competing brands. Given the administrative costs involved in large numbers of small market transactions, it is hard to imagine that such an information service would be offered exclusively by private firms through individual market transactions. Neither would potential suppliers of such information be very interested in such a market because they would know that the consumer who buys such information could so easily pass it on to others. Thus too little of this kind of information service would be provided relative to the benefit of it to consumers. These factors rationalise the involvement of government agencies in disseminating information on energy efficiency.

Certain aspects of a market's structure may lead to inefficiency. For instance, a firm with monopoly power may be able to fend off competition from a new technology. In some countries or local markets, suppliers of financial services may not face much competition and this can result in unnecessarily high interest costs for financing purchases of energy-saving equipment.

One can see that government action is likely to be warranted in the case of some market barriers and not in others. In some situations dealing with barriers in a pragmatic way can be a matter of making sure that normal aspects of market infrastructure (e.g., consumer-protection laws, laws of contract) are working well in markets for energy technologies.

Second-best Solutions to Market Failure

There is also a more general argument that favours some level of support for new energy technologies that reduce air pollutants and carbon emissions. The logic of the market failure argument calls for the internalisation of market externalities. For instance, higher taxes on fossil fuels to internalise the external costs of consuming them would encourage the use of better energy technologies. But it is quite unrealistic to expect governments to do this in relation to all externalities. Governments demand a high level of certainty about the results of such expensive policies before instituting them and it is very difficult to convince them of the benefits of internalisation, which will materialise gradually and in complex ways. This is especially so when the damages of externalities are not well understood (as in the case of climate change).

In such a situation other measures are legitimised. An alternative way to achieve some of the same effects is to have government support markets that would grow if the internalisation of externalities were to be achieved. Economists refer to this as a "second-best argument," meaning that certain interventions in the market may be desirable when the first-best solution of depending on efficient markets is not attainable.

This argument should itself be kept in perspective. It does not imply a *carte blanche* for government action in favour of technology market development. If one pursues the implications of the argument, the problems associated with 'picking winners' have again to be dealt with and, even when there is a consensus about some technologies being winners, the question of how much government resources should be applied to reducing market barriers must be decided. Addressing that question calls for the use of benefit-cost accounting in evaluating proposed market development programmes, a subject discussed further below.

Market Barriers in a Dynamic Setting

For purposes of theorising, economists usually formulate the market barriers and market failure argument in a static framework. That is, to simplify the analysis of normal behavioural and structural issues of the kind we have been discussing, they hypothesise that certain things that may be in motion over longer periods are for the moment held constant. This includes technological change and the preferences of consumers for goods and services. Here we need to discuss both of these things. We should be focusing attention on *dynamic* issues as well as *static* ones.

A particularly relevant dynamic issue is the 'infant-industry argument'. It can be viewed as an earlier version of the market barriers argument that came out of the literature on international trade: a new industry (or market) needs protection from its competitors in other countries because it needs time to get on its feet. This view earned itself a bad name in some circles because, in practical terms, once an industry had protection from international competitors it worked hard at keeping it, and was often successful. The result was a long period of protectionism and the inefficiency that results from it.

Fortunately the institutional framework for government involvement in developing markets for new energy technologies is quite different from that which led to protecting domestic industries from foreign competition by way of legislated tariffs. Most funding for market development programmes is not open-ended; it comes directly from government budgets and involves year-to-year approvals and auditing procedures. Programmes in support of specific technologies also tend to have various forms of 'sunset clauses', so that direct support for "infant technologies" will be eliminated when a market takes off or when the infant technology has had enough time to take off but demonstrates that it is not economically viable. There is evidence of this way of thinking in the IEA case studies.[28]

The infant-industry argument is important in this discussion because it indicates the potential for substantial positive externalities. A firm that invests in a learning investment produces knowledge that can potentially be used by other firms in the same industry or, depending on the nature of the new knowledge, in other contexts. Whether the knowledge constitutes an external benefit depends on the ability of the firm to claim proprietorship of it. It is not an externality if patents and other forms of protection allow the firm either to keep the knowledge for its own use or sell it at a market-determined value. If it cannot do either of these, the firm will tend to under-invest in learning investments. Such under-investment is another instance of market failure – the existence of an expected positive externality is another strong case for government support of learning investments.

Another dynamic issue that warrants attention is the influence that market activity has on consumer preferences and behaviour. The market model of economic theory pictures an efficient interaction between many competitive suppliers who cannot individually influence the operation of the market and many consumers, each of whom has a well-defined and constant set of tastes. This is often far from reality. For example, the idea that the sport-utility-vehicle arrived on the scene as a result of the automobile companies responding to independently determined demands for them is hardly credible. Energy markets are very often interactions in which the choices available to consumers and

---

28. See, for instance, the US study on unconventional natural gas exploration and development (CS16) and the Canadian case study on space and water heating and cooling (CS3). For further discussion of the infant industry argument as it relates to the case studies, see Kliman (2001), sec. 4.4.

the preferences they have in regard to these choices are very much influenced by product differentiation strategies and other marketing activities of suppliers. When this occurs, especially in combination with the external effects of energy production and use, there is a strong case for governments to be involved in helping to build workably competitive markets for new energy technologies; and especially a strong case for governments to disseminate information on the implications of consumer decisions for energy consumption.

Applying Economic Analysis

The above discussion indicates that the market barriers perspective has come to be interpreted as being about economic efficiency. Governments should undertake programmes that reduce market barriers to the economically efficient adoption of new energy technologies. Achieving this goal requires policy designers to apply the tools of economic analysis in a practical setting. In addition to the abstractions discussed above, the messy details of actual markets, technologies, consumer behaviour and other complex phenomena have to be dealt with. One would hope that the IEA case studies could provide some insight from practical experience on whether and how this is done.

The issue is whether the policy successes claimed by the drafters of the case studies make good sense in market terms. For instance, have policy measures been designed in ways that make use of market processes and thereby in a competitive environment lead to results that are cost-efficient? Does it appear that units of a new technology are being sold because policy measures have overcome market barriers, as distinct from sales merely being 'purchased' by way of generous subsidies to buyers? Does it appear that policy measures will lead to the evolution of sustainable unsubsidised markets? Is there evidence that the relevant market information possessed by buyers and sellers is being enhanced by the policy measures? Where the infant-industry argument is motivating a policy measure, will it be phased out in timely fashion?

With some exceptions, these specific questions are not addressed directly in the case studies; the template was not designed to produce data that feed directly into the economist's analytical models. However, the studies do contain material that provides relevant insights and the overall impression given is that those responsible for designing technology market development programmes in IEA countries have paid a lot of attention to these kinds of questions. There are various sorts of evidence of this in the case studies: the use of performance objectives in order to leave more finely-tuned choices about technologies and how to market them to sellers and buyers; the attention given to the subtleties of market organisation and infrastructure that must be developed or adapted and to linkages between markets for related products; sensitivity to the view that information processes often involve public goods; the use of pricing to achieve policy objectives; and the use of benefit-cost techniques and other forms of audit in the operation of policy-related programmes. These observations of course apply to varying extents among the cases reported on. There is also a sense that policy design has been affected by when and where a policy was instituted. Later policies have benefited from the experience of earlier attempts at similar measures and national differences in political culture appear to play a role. But overall a market-oriented perspective is reflected in many of the case studies, as illustrated by the following observations.

Performance Objectives

One indication that policy designers understand the advantages of performance objectives as a policy tool is their use of the procurement model. It offers a classic framework for using competitive market behaviour to hasten the development and adoption of better technologies. The policy makers write a list of specific objectives for the technology concerned; the objectives may be both technical, in order to better adapt a technology to particular market needs, and commercial, in the sense of putting in place a suitable approach to marketing the technology. The specification list is then put out in a competitive bidding process to equipment suppliers. The American report on expanding the market for compact fluorescent lamps (CS17), and the Swedish reports on high-frequency electronic ballasts (CS12) and heat pumps (CS13) indicate that procurement programmes can be highly successful. They also suggest that operating a successful procurement policy requires a lot of careful organisation.

Several other case studies contain illustrations of the use of performance objectives, including the Austrian Thermoprofit programme (CS2), the Dutch programme on domestic ventilation (CS9) and the American programme for unconventional natural gas exploitation (CS16). The Austrian programme involves energy performance contracting by building owners. The Dutch ventilation effort fits into a large framework defined by an Energy Performance Standard introduced in 1995. In the American case study on natural gas the authors note that, among the various lessons they learned from this policy experience, "Special purpose 'performance based' rather than broadly structured or 'input based' economic incentives are a key to success."

The desirable effects of performance objectives can be enhanced with the help of specially-designed market mechanisms. The Dutch policy on encouraging renewable sources of energy includes a tradable certificates scheme for the production of electricity from renewables. It started on a voluntary basis in 1998 and involved a set of targets for each distribution company for the amount of electricity they distributed derived from renewable sources. The producer of each unit of 10 000 kWh of electricity generated from renewables and delivered to the grid received a 'Greenlabel' certificate in addition to the electricity price. Distribution companies that did not distribute enough eligible electricity were able to meet their targets by purchasing these Greenlabel certificates from the generating companies. This leads to more competition in the supply of renewable-based electricity, favours the lower-cost suppliers and distributes the burden of subsidies for renewables more fairly. Operation of the policy has resulted in a new market for bio-energy. In 2001 the voluntary Greenlabel system was replaced by a similar certificate system established on a legal basis and the marketing of green energy to final consumers in a liberalised market has been introduced.

Market Infrastructure

To function effectively markets must operate within a framework that is suited to the types of goods or services being traded so that it can effectively facilitate exchanges between sellers and buyers. Many of the requirements are obvious, some are quite subtle. A variety of things are involved; e.g., networks with suppliers of intermediate goods and services, the boundaries between producers of different components of a good or aspects of an associated service (i.e., the extent to which production and distribution processes are vertically and horizontally integrated), appropriate contracts and other legal arrangements, information channels, accepted standards and taxonomies. Arrangements of these sorts develop and evolve over time; in established industries traditional ways of doing things become engrained.

All of this has important implications for market development programmes. A new technology may require new kinds of arrangements and the market may have to be built from the ground up. Alternatively the technology may become one product option in an established market, but choosing it may require new ways of doing things and it may be difficult to entice market actors to adjust to its presence. Vested interests in the old way of doing things can be an important factor.

There is much evidence that programme designers are sensitive to these structural needs. Some of the case studies focus on classic aspects of establishing better markets; for instance, by establishing lasting systems of dependable information for buyers. An example is the Danish labelling programme for buildings (CS4). The seller of a building must have an energy audit performed by an approved consultant before the sale takes place. This results in an 'Energy Label' for the building, which provides information on energy and water consumption compared to other buildings with similar use, and an 'Energy Plan', which documents the labelling information and sets out proposals for improvements in the building. The seller can make improvements before sale in the hope of getting a better price. In cases where that does not happen, the programme provides buyers with information on what needs to be done and a potential source of funds for doing it (the saving due to a lower building price). The overall effect is to make it more likely that market prices will reflect differences in energy efficiency.

The building sector is an especially good example of the need to pay attention to the nature of market structure. As noted in Chapter 2, it is very fragmented and this is in part the *raison d'être* for energy service companies, which provide specialised information gathering and analytical services for energy users. But the effective operation of the energy service market has itself been a challenge. The Thermoprofit programme (CS2), which originated in the Austrian city of Graz, was in part intended to improve the performance of energy service companies, while at the same time contributing to the overall effectiveness of information dissemination in the building sector. In various ways the Austrian case study reflects a sensitivity to the complexity of market processes and the need to find entry points for policy within existing market structures. It has taken existing energy service companies as a starting point and built them into a network. This facilitates information transfer, the availability of financial options, bidding procedures to assure cost controls, monitoring of results and certification. The inclusion of a quality label in the programme recognises the need to deal with market risk for building owners and introduces a potential for internal growth momentum, in the sense that more building owners and building-service consumers will become aware of the advantages of the programme as future transactions in building markets take place.

Programme Efficiency and Success

There is evidence in the case studies that much attention is now paid to designing programmes so that they will be cost efficient and monitoring them to ascertain whether cost targets and programme objectives are being fulfilled. This is reflected in the structure and organisation of programmes and in the use of *benefit-cost analysis* (BCA) of various sorts in managing programmes.

In regard to programme structure, one important decision concerns the boundaries of different programmes; i.e., the grouping of various market development activities into coherent and efficient programmes. This will be affected by the nature of the product markets being targeted, the technologies involved and the specific nature of programme objectives. We have already seen examples of how the nature of the target markets can influence programme organisation. The fragmented character of building markets has led programme designers to group together promotional and market enhancement activities associated with a range of building technologies and in some cases to base programme mechanisms on performance objectives. In other situations it can make sense to structure programmes around specific functional and process objectives. When certain activities – such as information dissemination and education – are being done in high volumes, it makes sense to set up specialised units that perform these functions for a range of technologies and markets. Three case studies indicate that this kind of specialisation can be carried far and can be very effective: the UK's Energy Efficiency Best Practice Programme (CS15) and two case studies from the US – the Motor Challenge and Best Practices Programme (CS20) and the Industrial Assessment Centers Programme (CS19).

The report on the UK's Best Practice Programme also draws attention to the use of benefit-cost techniques in programme management. It notes that the activities it needs to do to persuade target organisations to use cost-effective technologies and management techniques must provide a benefit of at least £5 per year in energy saving for every £1 of programme cost. It also reports independent estimates in 1999 of total energy savings in excess of £650 million per year and the expectation that the current target of £800 million will be achieved. Another case study that reflects the application of BCA is the already-cited US programme on natural gas exploration (CS16). The programme was run for the US Department of Energy by the Gas Research Institute, which was required by the Federal Energy Regulatory Commission to apply its benefit-cost techniques as a part of programme management.

BCA is part of this discussion because it is the economist's standard tool for evaluating government programmes in relation to efficiency in resource use, which is the central objective underlying the market barriers perspective. In this view, decisions on setting up programmes in the first place should be subject to a benefit-cost calculation and BCA should be used as a tool in the operation of programmes (e.g., to evaluate applications for grants in support of technology development or marketing). And if BCA has been used in this way, one might expect the approach to be used to report on the success of programmes completed or in operation. In some of the case studies this use of benefit-cost ratios to measure success is mentioned, but more often the reports refer primarily to physical measures as defined by programme objectives when discussing success (e.g., numbers of units of a new technology installed, numbers of energy audits undertaken, etc.). In general one can guess from reading the case studies that attempts at comprehensive BCAs have not been made in very many cases. Its use as a decision-making tool in the operation of programmes is probably more frequent, but in most of the reports there is not enough information provided to allow a judgement on how thorough the BCA calculations were.

In this regard it should be acknowledged that thoroughness in BCA can be very difficult because of the data requirements involved and that there are problems involved in its use in the present context. For instance, for a programme to reduce greenhouse gas emissions a classic BCA would include the assignment of monetary values for the benefits of emission reductions. Given the present state of knowledge, there would be a large element of arbitrariness in assigning such values. At the same time, one can be pragmatic about such limitations by taking as a starting point that the government has decided to pursue emission reductions and focus on the cost side of the calculation. That is, one can use physical measures defined by programme objectives to represent the benefit side and still be thorough about the calculation on the cost side. It remains necessary to base decisions on the size and other aspects of programmes on coherent procedures of some kind. The BCA framework provides a systematic and transparent approach for doing that. It is possible to use it in a pragmatic way that sensibly recognises the limitations of the overall analytical model.

It is also useful to draw attention to the scope for more use of econometric techniques. This can be useful as an aid in setting programme parameters (e.g., the size of subsidies), as part of more thorough BCA, or simply to understand how effective programmes have been. For instance, a key issue is how to unravel the effects of market development actions from market growth that would likely have taken place anyway. When levels of adoption of a technology have increased during a period in which a market development policy has been in effect, it cannot be automatically concluded that these increases are attributable to the policy. This is often implicitly acknowledged by the presentation of various forms of supporting evidence. However, that evidence is often anecdotal and can be difficult to evaluate. Though econometric techniques themselves involve complex interpretation, they have the advantage of being based on a systematic analysis of statistical data.

There is no mention of econometric investigations in regard to any of the programmes reported on in the case studies. In one respect this is not surprising, since they require large amounts of data that can be costly to collect. Thus their use is a matter of background research and special studies. There is a need to do more of it – in some situations econometric analysis can provide answers to exactly the kinds of questions that policy designers need to know.[29]

---

29. A recent study provides an excellent illustration of what can be done with econometric techniques. In his study of the "Green Lights" programme of the US Environmental Protection Agency, Horowitz (2001) not only shows that this effort in support of the diffusion of fluorescent lighting ballasts was a very effective policy, he was also able to compare its effects with more piecemeal demand side rebate programmes. He finds that "... it is far more cost-effective to attempt to transform a national market through long-term coordinated coast-to-coast efforts that permit market preferences to evolve and mature, than it is to temporarily manipulate local markets through piecemeal programs that are highly variable from place to place and from year to year. In short, persistent efforts to educate producers and consumers and inform them of energy efficiency benefits appear to be more capable of building sustainable sales volume and market share than the alternative of financial subsidies." (p.121)

Where to from here?

To summarise the above discussion, according to the market barriers perspective, government should do something about barriers when they involve market failure and beyond that leave technology deployment to the market. 'Doing something' involves internalising externalities by adjusting market prices or by making changes in the organisation and structure of markets, including the background framework within which they operate.

The standard way of adjusting market prices to internalise a negative externality is to levy taxes that will force sellers and buyers of products to take account of costs that are external to the market. In the case of positive externalities, such as those that flow from learning investments, the pricing approach to internalising them calls for subsidies. The classic price-adjustment approach to internalising externalities is a powerful tool in some situations and impractical in others. The question of whether and how it should be pushed further in the context of energy use is important, though a subject that is beyond the scope of this book.

Much of what we refer to as deployment or market development policies falls into the category of adjusting market structure so that markets will operate well in relation to new technologies. Economic analysis is very helpful in identifying in fundamental terms the aspects of market structure that need attention, but provides only part of the framework and analysis needed for designing and implementing policy approaches to improving it. The practical side of the effort requires a much more eclectic approach. That comes with the market transformation perspective, discussed in the next chapter.

CHAPTER 5: A MARKET TRANSFORMATION PERSPECTIVE

What is Market Transformation?

The term *market transformation* has a particular meaning in the context of energy policy; it refers to a significant or even radical change in the distribution of products in a given market, in which the most efficient products substantially displace the least efficient ones. A *market transformation programme* refers to actions taken by government (or sometimes by some other entity acting in the public interest) to facilitate the market transformation process. In effect, the long-term objective of most such initiatives is to make an energy efficient technology or product-type the preferred 'norm' in a market place, whereas a more typical efficiency-performance distribution of the various product brands available in a market is represented by a normal curve with a lower mean performance, as illustrated in Figure 5.1.

Figure 5.1: Effect of Market Transformation on Product Performance

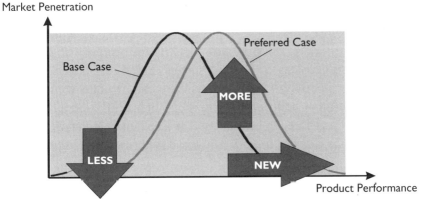

Source: Nilsson (1996)

As the use of the word 'transformation' suggests, the objective of a market transformation programme is to make changes that are both substantial and sustainable. An isolated instance in which a government supports the introduction of a new energy technology does not constitute a market transformation programme. Market transformation is about engineering substantial change in the market for a particular class of products: changes in the behaviour of consumers so that they choose to buy more efficient goods or services; changes in the behaviour of producers, so that they bring to the market only efficient (or at least more efficient) models; changes in the behaviour of wholesalers and retailers in regard to what they make available to final buyers; and changes in the capabilities of suppliers in related markets to provide whatever ancillary goods and services are needed (e.g., suppliers of equipment parts and other intermediate goods, installers, repair companies). When the process is completed, a successful market transformation programme will have had a lasting and significant effect.

An identifiable set of ideas about market transformation has taken shape over the last decade or so among people who have been involved in designing and implementing energy efficiency programmes. This includes contributions from people who have worked in demand-side management (DSM) programmes operated by electrical utilities.[30] As experience with the design of energy conservation programmes accumulated, practitioners began to see the need to make the results of their efforts more durable. To do this it was necessary to expand the horizons of their work, which tended to focus too narrowly on the energy end-use decisions of final consumers. Better results can be obtained by approaching the conservation issue in a broader context that takes account of both demand and supply in markets for the end-use equipment purchased by consumers. The idea took hold that those markets could be changed in ways that would lead consumers to more

---

30. Discussion of the development of ideas on market transformation can be found in Blumstein *et al* (1998) and other references listed there. Kunkle & Lutzenhiser (1998) report on case studies of market transformation as it evolved from its roots in the context of DSM.

often buy better end-use technologies, for example by working with equipment manufacturers to encourage them to market more energy-efficient products, establishing labelling schemes and taking other initiatives that affect the range of choices available to buyers as well as their knowledge base. By working on both sides of the market the potential for saving energy would be larger and the results more durable. These ideas spread and evolved and in the early 1990s a market transformation perspective began to emerge as a coherent framework for the thinking of those responsible for energy efficiency programmes.[31]

In this book the idea of a market transformation perspective is further expanded. In addition to its being a body of common understanding among those who work on energy efficiency policy and programmes, we see the market transformation perspective as fitting into a larger picture of what can be done by governments to help build markets for new energy technologies. In Chapters 3 and 4 we have shown how the R&D+Deployment and the market barriers perspectives are useful. In both cases, however, these perspectives draw limits around themselves. The R&D+Deployment perspective deals primarily with the implications of learning and the interactions between R&D and market development, particularly for the cost and performance of new technologies. The market barriers perspective identifies obstacles in the way of new technologies and suggests ways to deal with them that conform to the constraints of market economics, but does not deal in depth with how to implement change. Economic analysis is rich in insights about problems in existing markets, but does not say very much about the steps needed to tease new markets out of the entrepreneurial mechanism that creates them. In contrast, the emerging market transformation perspective focuses on the outcome to be achieved and then runs the logic back through all the factors that would be necessary to attain that outcome: improving technology cost

---

31. Of course, progress on the transformation of some markets for end-use equipment was made before the 1990s. For discussions of early efforts at market transformation, see Geller & Nadel (1994) and Tatutani (1995).

and performance and removing barriers, but also actively creating the conditions that facilitate the rapid market uptake of new more efficient products.

In a nutshell, the idea at the centre of the market transformation perspective is that people involved in technology deployment policy should think about what is needed to encourage the adoption of new products in the same way that private-sector suppliers think about it. That is, they have to understand in depth what makes the market for a new product take off, and then use that understanding to identify aspects of market structure and behaviour that affect product acceptance and also happen to be determined or affected by government actions. The idea is to apply the kind of expertise used by business to develop markets in pursuing the objectives of government policy in the energy sector. Unlike a business, however, the designer of a market transformation strategy is consciously pursuing a public policy objective; and therefore needs to exercise great care not to usurp the proper role of the market in 'picking winners' (and losers). They also must understand that market transformation actions involve risks; for instance, badly designed efforts could diminish choice and competition in the market, possibly leading to increased costs and a reduction in net welfare.

It is useful at the outset to recognise that there is a kind of tension between the market barrier perspective and the market transformation perspective. As we have seen in Chapter 4, the market barriers perspective has been formulated within the framework of neoclassical economics, which involves a strong focus on delineating the roles of government and decision makers in the private sector. Government has an important role, but the underlying value being promoted is that it should be kept to a minimum. This seems at odds with the very definition of the market transformation perspective, which assumes that governments should intervene to make markets work better. It is our contention – and both the IEA case studies and the background ideas discussed further in this chapter bear that out – that the two perspectives have to a great extent come to terms with each other and that the tension between them is quite healthy.[32] Market transformation programmes involve governments in influencing market decisions, but an important aspect of the market transformation perspective has come to be an emphasis on designing that influence so as to interfere with normal market processes as little as possible. The objective is to affect private energy-related decisions by reducing market barriers, changing incentive structures, providing public information, and encouraging competition in the aspects of products that determine energy efficiency and emissions. Good market transformation programmes are about raising the profile of energy variables in market activities and making once-only adjustments to the background infrastructure in which markets operate; and doing that in ways that are consistent with a public-good approach to policy making in a dynamic economy. It is not about regulatory tribunals, price controls and other forms of intervention that have been overly used and therefore discredited.

Doing Market Transformation

Developing effective market transformation policies is straight forward in principle, but far from easy in practice. The straight forward principle is first to develop an understanding of the buyer-relevant characteristics (both positive and negative) of the technologies being promoted and the workings of the markets that will potentially be transformed; and then to identify strategies that would help to boost the positive attributes (including high energy efficiency) and overcome the negative ones (e.g., high purchase costs, a lack of a proven track

---

32. This does not mean that the two perspectives are based on exactly the same assumptions – they are not. One illustration of differing assumptions is evident in the importance of the objective of changing consumer behaviour in the market transformation perspective. The market barriers perspective is closely linked to economic theory. The economist's analytical model normally takes consumer preferences as given, which does not encourage focusing on them as a primary target of policy. Thus the market transformation perspective should not be looked on as being only about implementing policies consistent with market barriers perspective; it reflects some differences in thinking.

record, etc.). The practice is far from easy because products and markets differ in ways that might be well understood by suppliers but will not be easily grasped by policy practitioners who arrive on the scene with quite different backgrounds. Furthermore, as noted above, care must be taken not to interfere with the normally efficient aspects of market-based resource allocation.

In large part this challenge is dealt with through diligent and open-minded interaction with people involved in the target markets and by an openness to a variety of expertise. Market transformation practitioners need to be wide-ranging and eclectic in regard to the bodies of knowledge they draw upon. A variety of disciplines are relevant, such as marketing, economics, psychology, management science and engineering; and experience in the target market is obviously a big plus when it comes to qualifying for a job on a market transformation project.

It is not realistic here to try to set out a recipe for doing effective market transformation at a general level. At the same time, it is useful to outline broadly the steps involved and to see how market transformation ideas enter the IEA case studies. All of the case studies involve some aspects of the market transformation approach, but to varying degrees. Table 5.1 puts the 22 cases into three categories.[33] Category 1 programmes (with a single + in the right-hand column of Table 5.1) have been primarily fashioned according to either the R&D+Deployment perspective or the market barriers perspective, but still have some elements of market transformation in them.[34] Programmes reported on in Category 2 (++) include several market transformation features; and Category 3 cases (+++) report on typical market transformation programmes. The assignment of cases to these categories admittedly involves some subjective judgement.

---

33. This section, and several other parts of this chapter, draw on the "Technologies Require Markets" Workshop paper by Lund (2001).

34. To illustrate how a project can be guided by R&D thinking or a focus on economic incentives but still have some market transformation elements, one can consider the development of photovoltaic power generation in Japan (CS8) and the Netherlands (CS10). Developing networks of communication and alliances with market actors figured importantly in both projects – a central feature of the market transformation approach.

The starting point for the development of market transformation programmes is to identify the technologies and the markets to be worked upon. Central to this is an evaluation of the potential for increasing societal welfare through government action. In the present context this means exploiting a potential for improving energy efficiency in a way that generates net benefit but would not be brought about by normal market processes, at least not as quickly.

Such unexploited potential may exist for various reasons. For instance, the technology to improve the energy efficiency of a given type of household appliance might be available but not yet incorporated to a significant degree into widely marketed models. Suppliers in that market might find their current range of models to be quite profitable; they might be aware of the possibility of improving energy efficiency without adding greatly to their production costs, but may not view its incorporation into their products as a high-priority option in their overall marketing strategies. This might involve a belief that consumers are more likely to focus on initial purchase costs and non-energy aspects of performance than to take account of energy costs over the product's life cycle. Indeed energy might contribute a relatively small portion to total life-cycle costs. In such a situation, a range of market transformation actions can be effective in tilting supplier strategies towards introducing the new technology. In a market with several suppliers it can be possible to do this by taking action that will focus competition on energy efficiency; for instance, with a combination of actions that reinforce each other, such as by working with suppliers through a procurement programme while at the same time enhancing the likelihood that buyers will pay attention to the energy-using characteristics of the appliance by way of an energy labelling system combined with advertising and sales training programmes. In other types of markets it may be necessary to intervene more aggressively to set the transformation in motion; for instance, by amending mandatory product standards.

In practice the market transformation practitioner has to deal with many complications because target markets can be very complex. Many energy services can be provided in more than one way and markets interact with each other and often disaggregate into systems of sub-markets. Thus even the initial step of specifying the market to be worked on has to be understood as an open process with feedback loops – all of the areas to be worked on may not become clear until after the work has begun.

Table 5.1. IEA Case Studies Categorised According to the Extent Market Transformation Tools were Used

Country	CS No	Case Study Title	Policies & Measures	MT
Austria	1	Deployment of biomass district heating	Niche management, subsidies and soft loans from national and state governments to agricultural cooperatives and biomass users	++
	2	Thermoprofit: Reducing energy consumption in buildings	Energy performance contracting, 3rd-party financing, information programme directed to enhancing performance of energy service companies, quality labelling	++
Canada	3	Renewable energy deployment initiative in space and water heating/cooling	Market assessments & strategy development, partnerships with industry associations, financial incentives	++
Denmark	4	Energy labelling for small buildings to save energy and water	Supply information to real estate markets by way of required energy audit prior to sale, labelling	++
Finland	5	Diesel engines for combined-cycle power generation	R&D, demonstration, Funding programme in partnership with industry	+
Germany	6	Solarbau: Energy efficiency and solar energy in the commercial building sector	R&D funding combined with demonstration programme	+
	7	Wind power for grid connection – the 250 MW wind programme	Experimental and operating-data-collection programme involving various types of subsidies, price incentives & feed-in compensation	++
Japan	8	Photovoltaic power generation – from R&D to deployment	Large government-industry partnership combining R&D, demonstration, standards, information dissemination, etc.	+

Table 5.1. IEA Case Studies Categorised According to the Extent Market Transformation Tools were Used (continued)

Country	CS No	Case Study Title	Policies & Measures	MT
Netherlands	9	Deployment of high efficiency heat recovery for domestic ventilation	Information, promotion & regulation programme, incentives; links to operation of overall energy performance standards in new buildings	+++
	10	Photovoltaic covenant	R&D, demonstration, information, through voluntary agreements, subsidies	+
	11	Deployment of renewable energy in a liberalised energy market by fiscal instruments	Differential taxes on conventional & renewable sources; 'green electricity' incentives; tradable-certificate scheme for electricity production	+
Sweden	12	Market transformation: lighting	Procurement, demonstration, information	+++
	13	Market transformation: heat pumps	Procurement with design/development competition, information dissemination	+++
	14	Environmentally-adapted energy systems in Baltic Sea region	Loan-guarantees, technical assistance to reduce emissions	+
United Kingdom	15	Energy efficiency best practice	Information dissemination, technical assistance, targeted advice, management consulting, etc	++
United States	16	Unconventional natural gas exploration and production	R&D, price & tax incentives, market reforms	++
	17	Sub-compact fluorescent lamps	Procurement, design/development comp., information, consultation with stakeholders	+++
	18	Clean coal technology demonstration	R&D, demonstration, procurement model with design/development competition	++
	19	Industrial assessment centres	Information, auditing, partners with universities	++
	20	Motor challenge and BestPractices programs	Information and decision-making tools, energy assessments, training, strategic partnerships with industry	++
European Union	21	Energy + procurement	Refrigerator/freezer multi-country procurement	+++
International	22	IEA/SolarPACES START Missions	Information, technology transfer	+

Once the scope of the exercise has been established in terms of the technical performance variables to be promoted and the products that are involved, the markets to be worked on are examined closely to identify all of the important decision makers according to the different roles they play. Table 5.2 illustrates that the number of different market players can be large and varied. While some of the roles played by market actors overlap and many actors have multiple roles, the table indicates that consulting with stakeholders, and involving some of them in the transformation process in other ways, is a large job. It is nevertheless a centrepiece of most market transformation programmes. The chances of having a performance enhancement or a new product accepted can be greatly increased through the involvement of important market players, especially when the changes are technically complex and currently accepted products are well established.

Working with stakeholders can be done by tapping into existing networks, such as trade associations and consumer groups, or by building new networks of contacts. For instance, in technology procurement programmes developing cooperative networks among buyer-groups is important. Industry associations may develop their own networks to work together on building the foundations for the offering of a new product.

Broad strategic choices are necessary early in the development of a market transformation programme. For instance, an emerging technology may be technically superior but still not price-competitive. Will the focus in such a case be on cost reduction or on competing through product differentiation? Or both in parallel? Technologies may not yet be well suited to satisfy the whole range of user needs. Will an effort be made to transform a large market or will the programme be limited to a market niche? In general, working in market niches offers less risk and they can be the starting points for larger efforts in the future.

In addition to dealing with these kinds of generic aspects of a market transformation programme, various broadly-defined models can be used

Table 5.2. Types of Market Actors Involved in Case Study Projects

Typical Role	Market Actor
Buyer	Facility operators
Buyer & seller	Distributors, wholesalers, retailers, purchasers, contractors, service companies, utilities, energy distributors
Development	Planners, architects
Development – manufacturing	Manufacturing companies, parts suppliers
Financing	Funding brokers & other financial institutions
Information dissemination	Energy agencies, mass media companies & agencies, individual investors
Policy & funding	Government agencies, other public institutions
Policy – formulation & decisions	Politicians, regulatory agencies & other public authorities
Represent special interests	Trade associations, consumer associations, other NGOs
Basic research	Universities
Research & development	Research institutes, corporate research labs
Seller	Equipment installers, energy distributors
Special tasks (e.g., policy analysis)	Consultants
Technology user	Homeowners, consumers, customers, end users

Source: Lund (2001)

Figure 5.2. Developing Networks for Market Transformation

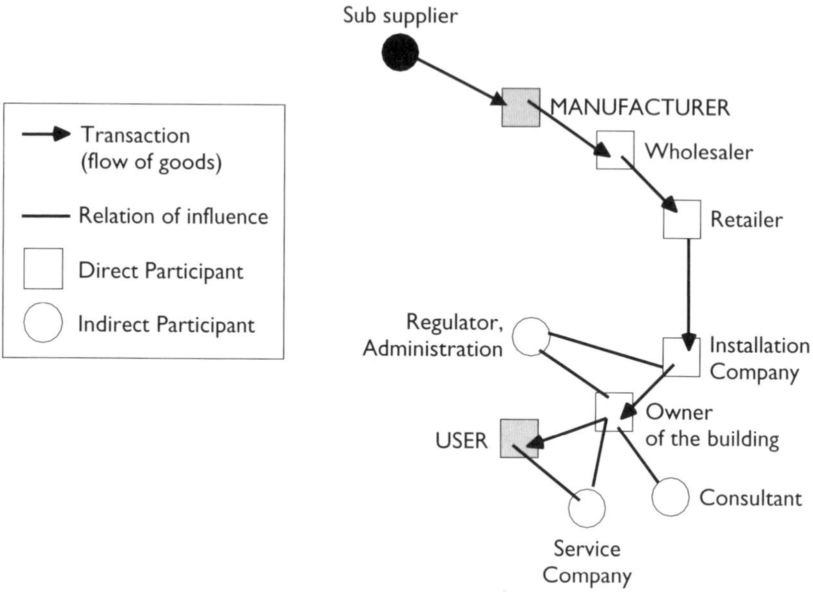

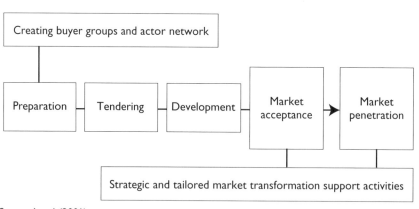

Source: Nilsson (1996).

Figure 5.3. Technology Procurement Process

Source: Lund (2001).

as the basis for developing a detailed plan. Three are briefly described here.

Procurement Actions

Procurement processes are a natural vehicle for encouraging technology market development – they offer an entry point for influencing industry decisions in a framework that governments know well. The case studies on procurement programmes have been cited in both of the two preceding chapters: in regard to the R&D+Deployment perspective to illustrate how policy can be used to encourage technology and organisational learning; and in regard to the market barriers perspective to show how market-linked tools can help to assure that policy objectives are achieved in efficient ways that leave technical decisions and resource allocation to the private sector. In the market transformation perspective, a procurement specification list provides a useful pathway for programme designers to get into the details of market operations.

Technology procurement can be viewed as a tool that can influence the whole chain of innovation and commercialisation. This requires multi-stage procurement programmes, as illustrated in Figure 5.3.

One strength of the procurement model is that it allows policy designers to deal with a thorny problem in end-use energy efficiency policy. How do you entice consumers to buy energy-efficient equipment when the cost of energy is only a small component of its total cost and the consumer is much more interested in characteristics of the equipment other than its energy efficiency? The answer is to entice equipment producers to embed energy-efficient technologies in products designed with other characteristics that consumers think are important. This is not high-level R&D, but it is an important bit of common sense. In the new products that resulted from the procurement programmes in the case studies, equipment suppliers were able to make improvements quite easily. However, prior to being nudged by the procurement programmes, they had little incentive to develop improved versions of their products that would substitute for existing versions that were already profitable. Procurement programmes arouse a latent potential and encourage new thinking that results in both technical and commercial development. This is illustrated by the US programme on sub-compact fluorescent lighting (CS17), which was a matter of developing bulbs that fit into a larger range of typical lighting fixtures, and the Swedish programme for high-frequency ballasts (CS12), which led to equipment with better lighting quality and increased productivity.

There is great potential for variety in the design of procurement programmes. One way to see that is by considering the spectrum of choices available along several dimensions that are involved in designing them.

- *Components vs systems:* The target technology may vary from specific components of a technical system to a whole system or facility. A single component may be a generic technology and widely applicable, whereas a system may have local features. A system may involve more flexibility and leave room for different approaches, whereas a component-approach is often tied to a certain technology. Risk and complexity increase when going from a single component to a system.

- *National vs international programmes:* Procurement programmes are usually arranged nationally but made open to competition from international manufacturers through national regulation and trade agreements. International procurement processes increase the purchasing power of buyer groups and more strict criteria can be applied.

- *Single-stage vs multi-stage programmes:* Most programmes are single projects based on one product specification. An interesting innovation would be to introduce a multi-stage process that builds on the strengths of a particular procurement approach. Some examples: the first stage might be national and the second stage international in order to multiply the effects of the programme and its appeal to suppliers; the first stage might involve a system component and the second the whole system; or the first stage might focus on working with manufacturers and the second with consumers.

■ *Externally-led vs self-organised programmes:* Technology procurement must be highly organised and carefully managed to be successful, which means that leadership is important. But some versions of the procurement model can take shape spontaneously. For example, it could arise when an established network of buyers comes to a voluntary consensus that a tendering procedure would benefit all members of the group. The Internet is a tool that might be effectively used to collect buyers and build purchasing power.

■ *Technology-focused vs ordinary procurement programmes:* The typical market transformation procurement programme has involved a strong focus on the technical characteristics of a relatively new product that requires some development to respond better to competition from established products. In an ordinary procurement programme, the focus may be on creating more purchasing power to reduce the price of better-than-average products.

Finally, it makes sense for a focused procurement programme to be associated with other market transformation actions that affect the market concerned. For instance, new information dissemination programmes and an energy labelling system might be timed to interact with the results of a procurement effort. Similarly the development of buyer-groups might be timed contingently to follow the successful completion of the technical development aspect of the procurement arrangement. This kind of staged approach relates to the subject of the next sub-section.

Strategic Niche Management

As noted in Chapter 3, a technology niche market is one that offers sellers some limited level of protection against competition from existing products and therefore provides some room for experimentation, trial and error, and product modifications. At the same time the new technology is embedded in a wider market. This provides the opportunity for a different kind of market transformation strategy. Though the market transformation initiatives that are well known in policy circles have focused on facilitating the market penetration of proven products, the model can also be applied to facilitating the transformation of an initial niche platform into a major market. The underlying argument here is based on the idea that niche markets help to set important processes of change in motion: interactive learning, institutional adaptation, networking and technical development efforts that are necessary for the wider implementation of a niche technology.[35] Thus a market transformation programme could accelerate this process by focusing on aspects of change that depend on government actions (such as adjustments to standards and codes, public information, etc.) and providing leadership in bringing users, suppliers and other market actors together in an interactive learning process. This sort of approach to market transformation programmes involves more risk, but could be important in areas that require difficult changes in market infrastructure.

When trying to create the market niche in which such a strategy may be applied, it would be important to require a good fit between the technology being launched and the expectations of the market. This requires close consideration of market characteristics by the market transformation practitioner in ways that parallel the approach of the firms launching the new product. For instance, it is important to choose a niche that takes full advantage of the merits of the new technology, to concentrate initially on a limited number of applications and work first in small geographical areas. Working with forms of the technology that have the potential for scale economies increases the chances of success and it is helpful to focus on customers and users who are demanding and likely to lead the market in adopting new products.

The experimentation phase of the niche strategy is very important, as it may determine the form of the more mature technology that will be the basis of a move to a larger market. It can be accomplished through the

---

35. For a fuller discussion of this strategy, see (Kemp, 1998).

series of steps outlined in Figure 5.4. Several iterations of this sort – and even several niche markets – may be necessary before a new technology is fully embedded in a market and the key actors are prepared to scale-up to a larger market. Part of the early planning in a market transformation programme should be consideration of what to do if the niche is successful. For example, scaling up sales levels will involve larger financial commitments and early attention should be paid to this need.

By chance the best examples of the application of strategic niche management in the case studies are found in renewables programmes, rather than in the types of end-use markets in which market transformation programmes have more typically been applied. The Austrian Biomass District Heating case (CS1) is one example; it also demonstrates the possibility for market transformation programmes to be initiated by people outside centralised government energy agencies. Its development started in the early 1980s as a bottom-up local activity and government support came later. Small local biomass district heating systems provided the market niche and the key actors were local promoters who both used and developed the systems. More than 500 plants have been installed. The Canadian Renewable Energy Deployment Initiative (CS3) is another example of a programme that focuses on promising niche markets and applications, though it is at a much earlier stage than the Austrian programme.

Figure 5.4. **Bringing New Technologies into the Market through a Controlled Experimentation Process**

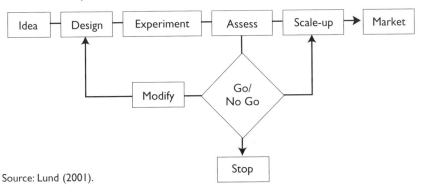

Source: Lund (2001).

Business Concept Innovation

An innovative business strategy may also provide a framework for market transformation policies of a different kind. In some parts of the energy sector traditional business models have involved little emphasis on innovation as a tool for creating competitive advantage; this can also be said about some other sectors of the economy in which large amounts of energy are consumed; e.g., the construction sector. An example in the energy sector is the traditional electric or natural gas utility, which in the past focused strongly on its core business. Regulatory regimes created a static environment that was not conducive to innovations in the products and services put on the market by these companies. Regulatory reform has changed that. In a more competitive environment, companies find that they have to pay attention not only to production efficiency and cost, but also to the specific needs of their target customer groups and to the more subtle characteristics of how they deliver their services. Thus an electricity company may find that it can attract end-use customers by offering a variety of services. E.g., household consumers may respond to the offer of maintenance services, information technology devices that improve household management or reduce energy costs, and 'green energy' packages. Industrial customers respond to time-of-use pricing, energy performance contracting or options to be involved in distributed generation facilities.

This suggests that there are situations in which market transformation techniques can be fit into or coordinated with regulatory reform. While the reform may be primarily motivated by other objectives, opportunities to achieve technology deployment objectives by encouraging new business concepts may take shape as part of the process of competitive change that is set in motion. Moreover one of the case studies indicates that the scope for government-industry cooperation on business concept development is not limited to areas of regulatory reform. CS5 reports on a Finnish project on the use of diesel engines for combined-cycle power generation. It involved support for the development of compact and modular combined heat and power systems by a major diesel equipment producer. Leading users and several providers of finance joined together to undertake a full-scale demonstration project. New ways of providing competitive energy solutions and total energy service concepts were developed. These have proven successful and have led to increased sales.

Facing the Challenge

Practitioners of market transformation policy clearly face a challenging task. They are expected to find ways to facilitate and hasten the incorporation of new energy technologies into industrial and commercial activities at a time when there is much suspicion about efforts by government to influence the economy. As a result they must treat their job as a matter of fine tuning. Ironically this can be viewed as a desirable state of affairs from the viewpoint of good public policy. The practical side of dealing with market barriers and supporting the emergence of markets for new technologies should not become another round of experiments in economic planning. At the same time, there is a necessary and legitimate role for government in building new markets because all markets work within a legal and institutional framework that is in part determined by government action and because there are important public-good effects associated with the increased use of cleaner and more efficient energy technologies.

In this light a clear guideline for the application of market transformation programmes can be proposed. When approaching markets in which there is an unexploited potential for net benefit to society through the expanded use of better energy technologies, the focus should be very specifically on ways to make the desirable energy-related attributes of the products involved more attractive to the suppliers and buyers of energy-related products and services, while at the same time disturbing normal market processes as little as possible. If this is done right, the forces of market competition will complete the job. It may appear as if market transformation practitioners are thereby being asked to walk an unrealistically narrow path. Happily there is evidence from a number of successful market transformation programmes that it is possible to find that path.

The idea of a market transformation perspective – one of the building blocks in the overall argument of this book – is in the early stages of its development relative to the other two perspectives we have discussed. It is a compendium of ideas that have taken shape out of the experience of policy practitioners and it is still evolving. It is nevertheless an important part of our discussion because it is about the details of getting the job of deployment policy done. There exist many opportunities to release the potential for cleaner and more efficient energy use. At a time when slowing or reversing the trend of energy consumption and emissions is a high-priority goal for government, the use of market transformation programmes to help release that potential can enhance societal welfare. The market transformation perspective and the craft that is necessary to mount successful market transformation programmes have been developing in response to this need.

CHAPTER 6: TOOLS FOR POLICY DESIGN

Whatever perspective may be motivating a market development programme, careful analysis is needed for designing it, obtaining funds for it, implementing it, managing it and understanding how well it has worked. In this chapter we survey some of the analytical issues associated with undertaking deployment policy. The first section describes some useful analytical tools and comments on them. The second section is a discussion of the challenges involved in evaluating programme impacts. Throughout the chapter we draw on ideas from the three policy perspectives as they are relevant.[36]

Analytical Tools

In this section three methods are discussed briefly: the use of a life-cycle framework in making decisions regarding energy efficiency, the use of experience curves to make rough estimates of subsidies needed to support learning investments, and the use of diffusion curves in developing market strategies. The intention is to illustrate the scope and need for using formal tools in a practical context.

Before proceeding to that, it should be acknowledged that some of the most important analytical requirements are not provided by formal analysis; and that this is confirmed by many observations in the IEA case studies. Sometimes there is no substitute for having a market situation analysed by people with appropriate experience and training

---

36. The theoretical frameworks associated with the three models determine to a large part their analytical approaches. The market barriers perspective is connected to a well-defined body of theoretical economic analysis. Besides the large literature on experience and learning curves, the R&D+Deployment perspective relies on methods developed in systems analysis and in research on innovation systems. The market transformation perspective relies on knowledge within management sciences and innovation theory, but being the most practice-oriented of the three perspectives, also pragmatically experiments with tools from other disciplines.

who have developed a keen eye for the practical side of their work. The most direct way to focus on marketing strategies for a new end-use technology may be to have a team of marketing specialists and applied psychologists look closely at the current market for the energy service involved. How the structure and organisation of an existing energy service market may impede the penetration of a new product might be most easily understood by a team made up of sales personnel from relevant firms assisted by an applied economist.

The case studies provide illustrations of the importance of drawing on established expertise and practical experience. For instance, the American procurement programme for sub-compact fluorescent lamps (CS17) shows how a market transformation team, in consultation with market stakeholders, was able to come up with practical solutions for some of the classic market barriers. To deal with product risk, the programme required manufacturers to offer an unconditional one-year warranty. It also dealt with the classic problem of building owners making key decisions affecting lighting, but typically not having to pay its operating cost and therefore undervaluing energy efficiency. Common-area outdoor lighting, for which building owners often pay the operating costs, was made part of the product specification for the sub-compact fluorescent lamps (sub-CFL); this enhanced the likelihood that building owners would be interested in the product.

At the same time, those who work on market transformation would undoubtedly agree that analytical tools of the sort discussed below are useful in their work.

Life-cycle Cost and Yield Calculations

Many energy consumers – especially householders, who use small amounts of energy – under-invest in energy efficiency because they are not aware of relevant opportunities or judge them to be too insignificant. When they make purchase decisions they often use simplified rules-of-thumb, which can be biased against rational decisions.

Table 6.1. Increases in Yields on an Investment for Years of Useful Life Longer than the Payback Time Required

		Useful Life of Equipment (Years)							
		3	**4**	**5**	**6**	**7**	**10**	**12**	**15**
Payback time required (years)	**2**	37%	79%	120%	159%	196%	300%	361%	444%
	3	–	14%	40%	65%	88%	154%	194%	247%
	4		–	0%	18%	35%	82%	111%	149%
	5			–	–	3%	40%	61%	91%
	6					–	12%	29%	53%
	8	Unprofitable						–	7%

Calculated under the assumption that the purchaser requires 15% return of capital and that inflation is 2%.

A classic example is the comparison of initial equipment costs when choosing from among alternative technologies, rather than full life-cycle costs. Another is the use of a short payback period as a purchase criterion, instead of calculating the expected net yield on a piece of equipment and comparing it to the opportunity cost of funds used for the expenditure. Manuals and textbook treatments of these kinds of calculations are easily accessible, as are illustrative analyses involving actual equipment.[37]

The effect of using inaccurate numbers and overly simple decision rules can be large. Table 6.1 illustrates the effect of using a payback period that is shorter than the useful life of a piece of equipment. For instance, in the illustration, if a consumer rejected a piece of equipment because it would not pay back its purchase price in two years when the

---

37. See, for instance, USDOE (2001).

equipment would in fact last for five years, the return on the investment foregone would be 120 percent higher than the two-year return. Figure 6.1 summarises the effect in a graph.

Figure 6.1. 'Multiplication' of yield on an investment that would have been rejected by the application of low pay back times but has long useful life times

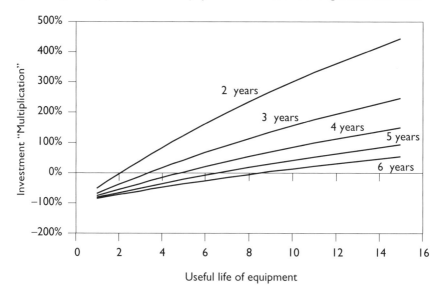

Experience Curves

Experience curves can be used to make rough estimates of subsidies needed to support learning investments on the way towards the take-off of a technology in commercial markets. Figure 6.2 shows the results of a simulation analysis based on Japan's market development programme for residential photovoltaic (PV) systems.[38] The investment curves in the graph are based on assumptions regarding the programme, the markets involved and the learning rates for PV modules expected. The points up to the year 1998 are based on

---

38. For a detailed description of the programme, see IEA (2000), 64-74.

observed data; the points after that are the result of a simulation exercise (using Japanese budget forecasts for 1999 and 2000).

Figure 6.2. Investments and Subsidies in PV-Roof Programme

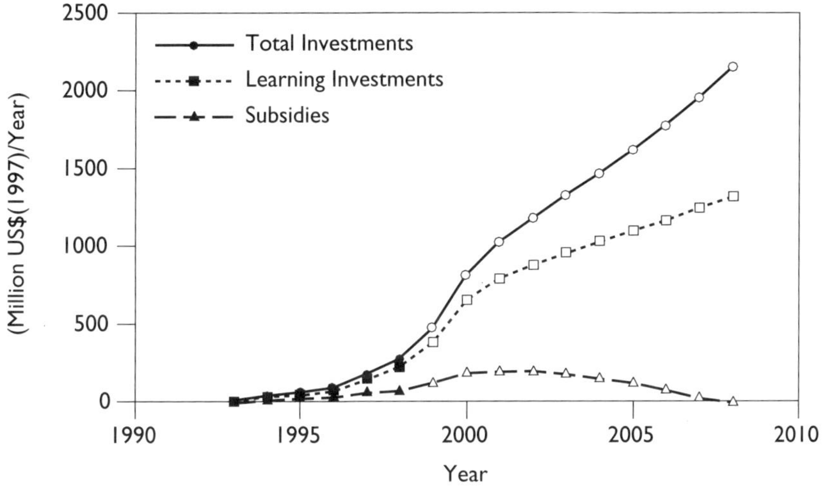

Source: OECD/IEA(2000)

When this niche market programme was started in 1993, the costs of residential PV systems were considerably higher than the buyers' willingness-to-pay and sizeable subsidies were required for the first units (consistent with the illustration set out in Chapter 3, Figure 3.5). As cumulative sales rise, the unit cost falls and subsidies for each unit can be reduced. However, in this simulation, volume grows faster than unit subsidies decrease and the total cost for the programme increases. As the programme expands, the initial 70 percent growth rate decreases and beyond 2002 cost reductions overcome sales growth. Prospective market investigations and extrapolation of the observed niche market curve are consistent with the experience curve for this PV-system reaching the point at which a niche market would be viable at around a system cost of 3 US$/Wp. The technology would then have reached the point at which the government's contribution to learning investments can end. With the assumptions used for Figure 6.2, this would happen in 2007. At that time, the government programme would have initiated a market with an annual sales volume of 2 billion US$. That market would involve additional learning investments that could provide the basis for a continued ride down the experience curve.

In sum, this example illustrates how experience curves can be used to estimate the need for subsidies, the scenario for reducing them and finally phasing them out.

Using the Diffusion Model

The idea that the adoption of successful new products by buyers throughout an economy grows according to an S-shaped curve has long been used in the study of innovation.[39] It is a useful tool for the analysis of market transformation programmes. For instance, it can be used to build a structured view of consumer attitudes that is helpful in developing marketing strategies and in understanding deployment policy. This is illustrated in Figure 6.3.

This structure could be mapped onto the niche market curve discussed in the preceding section. The 'Innovators' would then correspond to the first part of the niche market curve, where the buyer has a large willingness to pay for the new technology. An interesting illustration of the use of diffusion curves for analysing deployment programmes is found in Lund (2001, Sec. 6), where it is applied to Case Study 12, the Swedish programme on electronic ballasts.

Success has Many Faces

The aim of deployment programmes is naturally to bring about a lasting impact on the market for some sort of equipment. How to measure that impact and how to evaluate whether a programme can be viewed as successful is a multi-layered complicated question, one that warrants a book of its own. In this section our intention is not to

---

39. See, for example, Rogers (1995) and Moore (1991).

Figure 6.3. Who will buy and why?

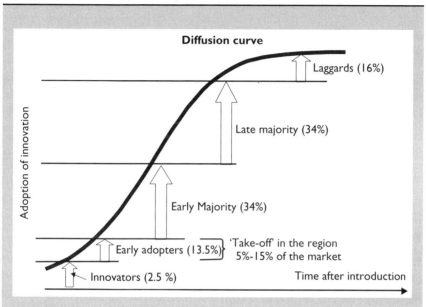

Adopter type	Characteristic	Role and size
Innovators • enthusiast	Venturesome; Enjoys the risk of being on the cutting edge; Demands technology	Market drivers. Want more technology, better performance. (16%)
Early adopters • visionaries	Well connected; Integrated in the main-stream of social system; Project oriented; Risk takers; Willing to experiment; Self-sufficient; Horizontally connected and acts as their peers	
THE CHASM (where marketing and distribution must radically change)		
Early majority • pragmatists	Deliberate; Process oriented; Risk Averse; Want proven applications; May need significant support; Vertically connected and acts as their superiors	Followers on the market. Want solutions and convenience (68%)
Late majority • conservatives	Sceptical; Does not like change in general. Changes under 'pressure' from the majority.	
Laggards • sceptics	Traditional; Point of reference is 'the good old days'; Actively resists innovations	Economic/ power interest different from status quo?

try to unravel it in any definitive way, but rather simply to survey some practical issues involved in it.

The template for the case studies on successful deployment programmes that provide the empirical basis of this book did not prescribe how to define success. Thus the guidance on this question offered by the studies themselves is mostly a matter of sampling the views on what constitutes success in ten different national capitals. Though that is of some interest, the issue here is methodological. What are some typical variables used to measure the impact of programmes and how should they be interpreted? To get a feel for the answer, we describe several ways that policy analysts measure programme impact and then discuss what they mean.

Volume Growth

To illustrate the simplest approach to measuring success – growth in the volume of sales – we look at some numbers from the worldwide market for compact fluorescent lamps (CFLs).

Establishment of a market for new products takes considerable time. The CFL has been a target product for many deployment activities throughout the last decade. As shown in Figure 6.4, accumulated output of CFLs has doubled almost six times between 1988 and 1999. Yearly sales for 1999 are in the order of 500 million units worldwide, which represents a tenfold increase in annual sales since 1988. It is believed that the total amount installed is some 1300 million units (IAEEL, 2000).

In spite of the impressive volume growth, the penetration of national markets is generally low. The total volume of light bulb sales is estimated to be in the range of 10-15 billion units per year, which means that CFL sales have a share between 0.5% and 3%.

Across the European Union the average number of light bulbs in households is 24. Table 6.2 shows the percentage of households that have a CFL and the average number per household; the data are mostly from 1995 (Palmer and Boardman, 1998). Given the low penetration of CFLs in households that own any (a bit above 10 percent), overall market penetration in these countries is on average less than 5 percent.

How much of a new technology will the market accept; what is the level of saturation? Tests of the suitability of CFLs for household

Figure 6.4. Worldwide Sales of CFLs

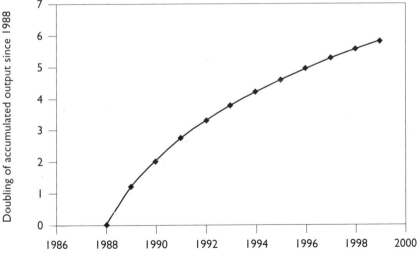

purposes with the present configuration of fixtures and lighting show that an average of eight light-bulbs could be comfortably replaced with CFL bulbs (Palmer and Boardman, 1998). If we assume this as the saturation level and apply a diffusion curve to the present level of market penetration as shown in Figure 6.5, it indicates that full dissemination would occur only after some 30 years.

Table 6.2. CFL Ownership in the European Union

Country	Households with CFL (%)	Average CFL per household	CFL per owning household
Belgium	29	0.9	3.7
Denmark	46	2.0	4.4
Finland	-	1.0	-
France	-	0.5	-
Germany	51	2.1	4.3
Greece	11.5	0.1	1.0
Ireland	22	0.9	4.0
Italy	55	1.1	2.0
Netherlands	62	2.7	4.5
Spain	11.5	0.2	1.7
Sweden	10	0.4	4.0
UK	23	0.7	3.0
EU average	32	0.9	2.8

Volume Growth and Price/Cost Trends

When a new product reaches the market and gets accepted, demand growth will bring about reductions in unit costs as scale economies are

Figure 6.5. Projected Growth of CFLs

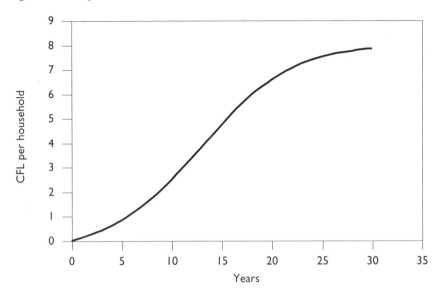

realised and new producers enter the market. This phenomenon is part of the learning process discussed in Chapter 3 and is captured by learning and experience curves. Movements along these curves provide another way of measuring the impacts of deployment programmes – an important way, because falling unit cost is associated with the promise of further growth.

The 'progress ratio' is a parameter that summarises the relation between cumulative output and the level of price or unit cost (depending on which of these variables has been used to construct the experience curve). This ratio indicates how much the cost or price will drop with each doubling of the cumulative production.[40] For example, if cumulative output doubles along a curve with a progress ratio of 84 percent, the cost or price will have dropped by 16 percent. Figure 6.6 shows the relation between the cumulative production of PV

---

40. The terms 'progress ratio' and 'learning rate' are both used in the literature to describe the slope of the experience curve. Learning rate = 100 – progress ratio. For additional discussion of the progress ratio and other aspects of experience curves, see OECD/IEA (2000).

modules and their price from producer to wholesaler. The strong reduction in this price between 1984 and 1987 reflects a drastic change in annual growth rates of module sales in this period from 56 percent per year to 16 percent per year.

Depending on how a market is organised, it can be difficult to perceive the effect of the learning process on costs until considerable time passes. Data that allow unit costs to be closely tracked are not generally available. Normally only the price can be observed. Early producers may be able to keep the market price from falling along with unit costs to recover their development costs and earn profits. If they can, it may not be clear how much unit costs have fallen until competition, actual or perceived, brings pressure for price reductions. Figure 6.7 illustrates this effect and also how the experience curve can be used to define various stages in the market introduction process that can be used in setting targets for deployment programmes and evaluating their effects.

Attribution of Impacts to Policy Measures

Before proceeding to other frameworks for evaluating the success of policy measures, it is important to acknowledge a key issue in the discussion: judging whether a market expansion that occurs after a programme has been implemented is actually a result of the measures taken, or one that would have occurred anyway. In some cases the attribution of an increase in sales to a deployment programme appears obvious; for example, when an entirely new product has been introduced by a firm that has developed it as part of a government-supported programme. But even in that kind of case attribution requires analysis and is in principle a matter of judgement, not fact. One cannot know how history would have unfolded in the absence of the programme – the company launching the new product, or some other company, might have ended up putting the product on the market by way of a different path, one that did not depend on government support.

From the vantage point of people working on deployment policy these kinds of questions are to some extent academic, especially when it

Figure 6.6. Market Changes for PV Modules, 1976-1996

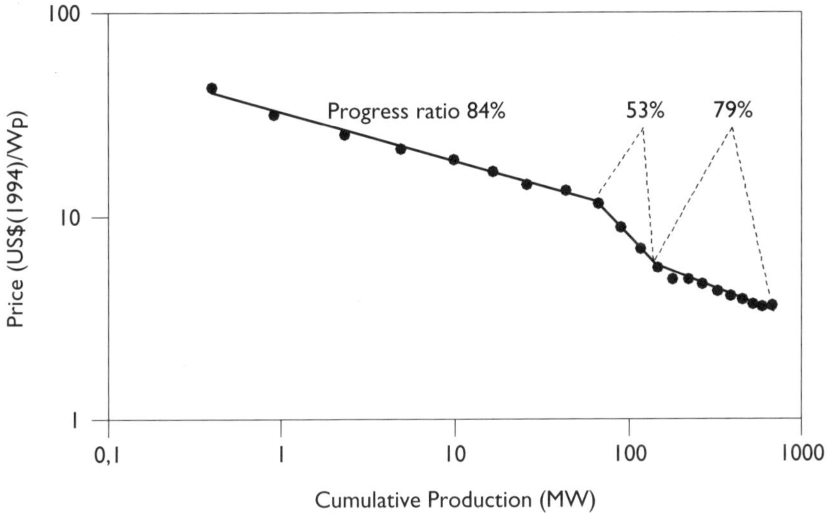

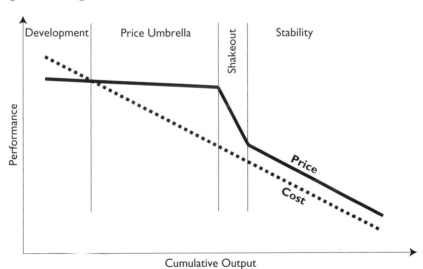

Source: OECD/IEA (2000)

Figure 6.7. Stages in a Market Introduction Process

Source: Boston Consulting Group (1968)

comes to discussing causality at a fundamental level. If a government is committed to supporting the deployment of new technologies, the officials who mount programmes in order to implement policy objectives have to take a practical approach to monitoring their work and evaluating whether it has been successful. Various kinds of analysis can be applied in order to make judgements that inspire confidence.

The most ambitious and convincing kind involves formal statistical analysis, in which attempts can be made to identify all of the variables that influence measures of market growth and understand how much of an observed change in them can be attributed to policy actions. It is important in this regard that specialisations in applied statistics have developed in a variety of disciplines relevant to deployment policy. Empirical analysis of the economic aspects of policy can be approached by econometricians; behavioural aspects can be studied by psychometricians, and so on.[41] The advantage of approaching evaluation in this way is that it brings much more than the minimum results necessary for "satisfying the Treasury upstairs that our policies are working". Statistical analysis can provide valuable information on consumer response to products, cost relations, externality values and other difficult aspects of policy design. The disadvantage is that it is time consuming and costly; and some types of analysis cannot even be approached without prior investment in the collection of dependable data.

Thus more pragmatic, simpler approaches to policy monitoring of the types described above and below remain important. Officials directly involved in the design and implementation of policy measures need feedback on their work that arrives more quickly and readily than the

---

41. As noted in Chapter 4, footnote 29, an example of a useful econometric study is Horowtiz (2001). Another example of relevant current work in econometrics is a set of papers given at the North American Conference of the International Association for Energy Economics in Vancouver, 6-8 October 2002, at a session entitled "Assessing the impact of energy conservation and energy efficiency efforts using discrete choice-related methods". Two of the papers are available on a CD-ROM Proceedings; see http://www.iaee.org/en/publications/proceedings.asp. On this subject, see also http://elsa.berkeley.edu/~train/.

results of major statistical studies. To deal with the attribution issue in a practical context it is frequently necessary to approach the interpretation of changes in market variables in a pragmatic way – with common sense, a critical eye, and as much supporting information as possible.

An illustration of a practical approach to programme monitoring is provided by a separate analysis of one of the programmes covered in the case studies (CS12). Neij (1999) reports on interviews with participants in the Swedish programme of support for high-frequency ballasts. Her findings indicate that the most important reason for buyer-interest in the new lighting fixtures had to do with lighting quality, rather than with energy efficiency. This sort of result adds credence to the hypothesis that the programme contributed to market growth that occurred after direct support from subsidies ended.

Performance Improvements

Much technological advance has its effect by way of gradually improving the performance of existing products. In these cases there is not a discernible new market to be developed, but rather the evolution of well established markets. To a great extent performance improvements · are made naturally through the process of competition, but in many instances actions by government play a role in the change. Thus the impact of deployment programmes through this channel also has to be considered.

Most programme activity of this kind that needs to be monitored falls into three categories:

- Government support spurs innovations that lead to performance-enhancing technologies;

- Government activities help to focus consumer interest on better versions of a product, leading to increased sales;

- Government takes action to discourage the purchase of products that under-perform, leading to decreased sales.

Trends in the sales of household appliances in Europe provide an illustration of the kind of information needed. Figure 6.8 shows that sales of cold appliances during the 1990s drifted from lower to higher performance levels (OECD/IEA, 2001). It is believed that energy-labelling and other programmes contributed to these trends.

Figure 6.8. EU Cold Appliances Sales by Energy label

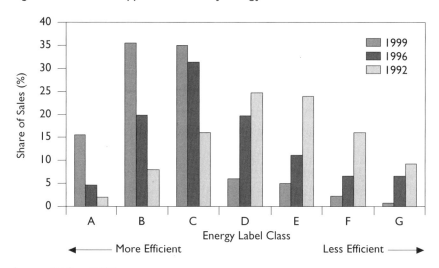

Source: EU-Save (2000)

This is a good example of a set of data that needs to be analysed econometrically with a view to estimating the portion of the trend toward higher performance that can be attributed to deployment programme activities and the portion that would have happened anyway. Such analysis would need to test for possible 'rebound effects' on energy consumption that can offset the hypothesised positive effects of deployment actions.

Benefit-Cost Analysis

None of the approaches to evaluating the success of a deployment programme discussed above is comprehensive. In each case a variable that is viewed as the 'output' of a programme is defined and then it is a matter of keeping track of that variable and collecting associated information that allows one to interpret its movements. This is often a correct approach for the management of a programme, but it is limited in relation to making decisions about funding programmes in the first place or doing *ex post* overall programme evaluations. A more comprehensive approach is generally needed for these purposes. The usual recommendation in this regard is to apply benefit-cost analysis. Since this was discussed in the section on "Programme efficiency and success" in Chapter 4, it is mentioned here only for the sake of completeness and to note that many useful sources on the nature, strengths and weaknesses of BCA are available.[42]

Summary Comments

Whatever is the aim of a programme and the chosen measure of success, the following practical observations are relevant in shaping it and in establishing evaluation procedures:

■ The attribution of impacts to measures is a matter of judgement that requires analysis;

■ Good monitoring procedures should be in place early in the life of a deployment programme;

■ Product innovations often lead to new behaviour from both users and producers;

■ Unit cost reductions might not be detectable, only price responses can be objectively measured;

■ The initial stage in the diffusion of an innovation through a market can be slow to materialise;

■ Total impact takes a lot of time.

---

42. See, for instance, Kopp, Krupnick and Toman (1997).

CHAPTER 7: LOOKING AT POLICY-MAKING FROM MULTIPLE PERSPECTIVES

In the introduction to this book we noted the difficulties involved in drawing lessons from case studies that are very dependent on particular contexts. To respond to that challenge we proposed an analytical framework based on three perspectives, which have been described in Chapters 3-5. The discussion in each chapter shows how that particular perspective can help to throw light on the case studies. In this chapter we try to take account of all three perspectives simultaneously.

We refer to our methodology as *triangulation* – by analysing a programme from three different directions it should be possible to understand it better (Nilsson and Wene, 2002). This approach has helped us to rise above the details of the individual cases and instead focus on the thinking behind policy design and implementation. For each study, we identified the aspects of policy-making and programme design that are linked to the key factors of each of the three perspectives. We kept track of these categories of programme characteristics on large worksheets and used them to look for patterns and develop speculative hypotheses. This sifting through details and the subsequent survey of a large 'map' of the case studies allowed us to approach some key questions in a way that accounted for all the perspectives together. For example, how do the different perspectives enter into the process of developing a programme? How do the aspects of a programme that relate to the different perspectives interact in support of programme objectives? What are the factors that make a deployment programme succeed?

In the larger sense, this kind of analysis is a work in progress. It is not realistic to expect clear answers to these hard questions based on the set of case studies we have in hand. However, we found that our approach helped us to draw some lessons from the experience reported on in case studies that are transferable across different contexts. The most important lesson of this kind is that different perspectives can lead to different results. While that observation should be evident from the discussion of the individual perspectives, we also draw it to your attention in the first section of this overview chapter by illustrating how a given policy measure can be viewed differently according to the perspective of the viewer. We then proceed through the steps of the triangulation analysis: first by reviewing some key aspects of the case studies from the viewpoint of each perspective individually and then by showing how the perspective-based views of deployment policy can be repackaged into a more holistic framework. We suggest that it is useful to attempt to synthesise the three policy perspectives discussed in this book in order to develop a more comprehensive approach to the analysis, design and implementation of deployment policy.

Policy Measures Viewed from Three Perspectives

It is clear from the discussion in Chapters 3-5 that each of the three policy perspectives has evolved in a particular setting, very much conditioned by the professional backgrounds and activities of the people involved in policy analysis and programme design. Thus it is not surprising that the issues surrounding the deployment of new technologies and the policies used to deal with them are viewed differently according to which perspective is favoured. This can affect how a policy measure is designed and used, which in turn can affect its results and one's evaluation of its success or failure. It is a matter of interest not only because it helps us to interpret case study material, but also because it might lead to insights on making better policy.

Because differences of interpretation of this sort are about the details and the nuances involved in policy measures, the point can be most easily conveyed by some hypothetical examples. Consider first how people coming from three different vantage points are likely to view the use of a subsidy to further the deployment of a new technology, as summarised in Figure 7.1 below.

Figure 7.1. Differing Interpretations of a Deployment Subsidy

Perspective	Function of the measure SUBSIDY
R&D + Deployment	The money should be used for investments in learning. The focus is on new products, technology characteristics and manufacturers that can move the process along. The subsidy is viewed as creating a future return in forms that cannot be predicted now. Success will be achieved when the market accepts the product on its own merits, taking account of both price and performance.
Market Transformation	The money should be used to attain interest from certain groups that could move the market. These groups are assumed to set trends and act as proponents for the improved products. The return from the subsidy is expected to come from the establishment of new preferences on the part of buyers and more interest on the part of suppliers in the business opportunities that can be created by exploiting a new technology.
Market Barriers	The money should be used to overcome a reluctance to buy new products that are superior to currently favoured products in ways that are not recognised by consumers, perhaps because they tend to over-estimate the risks involved in using the new product or because some of the benefits accrue to third parties. All customers are addressed equally. The money is spent in the public interest as viewed by the present value calculations of current buyers.

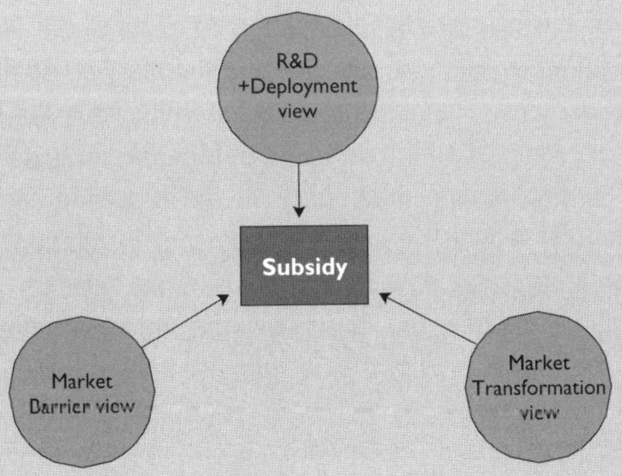

All three views of the subsidy characterised in this illustration are legitimate within their own frameworks, but each framework involves different assumptions and different views about what is important. The R&D+Deployment view starts from a position of confidence in the promise of a technology and a belief that it is necessary to try it out in order to make it work in a market context. The market transformation view reflects a parallel confidence in believing that a technology (presumably a different one, since it is ready for the market) is worthwhile for society and wants to find ways to convince others of that. The proponents of the market barriers view are more concerned with choosing the right thing to support, but tend to approach that issue in a narrow framework. In that sense they have something to learn from the other two perspectives. On the other hand, for the proponents of both the market transformation and R&D+Deployment perspectives to be successful, they too must apply some version of a net-value calculus; that is, they must choose the right consumer groups and the right technologies to subsidise if their efforts are to succeed.

Many other credible examples of this sort can be constructed. Three additional ones are presented in Table 7.1.

Perspective-based Observations

The first step in the triangulation analysis has been the thorough consideration of the case studies in relation to each of the individual perspectives separately. Here we set out some summary observations on these separate analyses. The objective is to see which issues 'bubbled to the top' when one looks at all the case studies together. This is based on a detailed accounting of individual policy measures cited in each of the studies. By identifying which issues are important in relation to each perspective we can then see how combinations of measures can be built up. This in part provides the basis for the more comprehensive perspective on deployment policy that we propose later in this chapter.[43]

---

43. The discussion in the three subsections that follow is helpful in understanding the types of policy measures referred to by way of shorthand labels in Table 7.3.

Table 7.1. Differing Interpretations of Deployment Measures – Additional Examples

Model	Information Dissemination	Tax-based Measures	Rules & Regulations
R&D + Deployment	Information is developed that will show how a particular technology, perhaps from a particular manufacturer, performs better than conventional technologies. Potential manufacturers may be the target for the information, rather than final users. Typical example: a demonstration project.	A tax-reduction is an incentive to develop an application or to adapt an industry to a new pattern of behaviour. The technology involved might be well-proven but the industry is risk averse or organised in such a way that a strong incentive is needed to stimulate private learning investments.	Rules are applied to define business standards and organisational behaviour and thus provide a robust framework for continuous technology learning. Administrative rules are used in order to secure fair competition and facilitate communication about agreements. Purchasing routines are a typical application and so is the use of quality assurance and environmental certification.
Market Transformation	The information focuses on performance ratings and is designed to reach customers when they are in the process of choosing a product. Typical example: labelling.	A tax or the rules for application of taxes could be used to punish the use of energy-inefficient equipment. Typical cases: special adjustments to property taxes, taxes on emissions.	Standards define how a product should perform and which of its functions are to be guaranteed. Compliance with building codes is an important example.
Market Barriers	The information deals with a broad range of characteristics of a product with a view to enabling the customer to make a better choice and calculate its consequences. Customers are informed in a general way and without specific products in mind. Typical case: bill inserts about energy efficiency sent by electric utilities to their customers.	Taxes should be as neutral as possible in terms of how they influence resource allocation. However, they can be used to correct prices that do not account for externalities and market imperfections.	Rules provide the framework for market activities in a manner that enables consistent transactions and assures entrepreneurs that certain things that affect risk are known. Rules often need to be legislated; enforcement to uphold fair competition may be necessary.

Barriers as Theories and Facts

Market barriers in the way of adoption of new energy technologies are mentioned frequently in the case studies (and the standard list of barriers, along with typical policy measures used to deal with them, is found in Table 4.1). Within the market barriers perspective, one can sometimes get the impression that it is only necessary for programme designers to devise measures that will reduce or eliminate the barriers; when these measures are implemented, rational participants in the markets concerned will embrace the new technologies without any more effort from the policy-maker. Getting beyond this theoretical position, the case studies provide evidence in support of the contention made at the end of Chapter 4 – that the barrier concept is useful for diagnosis of the problem, but is often very limited in regard to constructing specific programme measures. The latter point motivates the market transformation perspective. In sum, the economist's characterisation of markets is useful but very spare; it assumes that people behave homogenously according to strict rationality and constant preferences; and gives too little attention to how those preferences are formed and change.

The case studies indicate that policy designers draw in ideas from the market transformation perspective when dealing with market barriers. In some cases this is obvious, as in those describing bidding processes for the procurement of specified technologies. But market transformation ideas are also found in the descriptions of other programmes that did not come specifically from an application of the market transformation perspective.

Whether the ideas come from the market transformation perspective or elsewhere, the case studies taken together present a very clear indication that experience matters. Programme designers have moved from overly-simple depictions of market barrier remedies to more nuanced measures through trial and error. The studies show that successful programmes develop over time; designers acquire a deeper understanding of the problems they are dealing with and they fine-tune programme measures accordingly. Once again, there is learning-by-doing in policy-making!

Some market barriers were referred to in the case studies more often than others. The inertia involved in traditional market organisation is mentioned often. This is important, because it indicates how incumbent technologies are fortified by institutions that have developed in response to their characteristics. It illustrates again how the identification of a type of barrier does not in itself give sufficient information on which market actors could be the champions of a change, and with which arguments. What is needed to deal with this kind of barrier is organisational learning based on the particular contexts of the old and new technologies. The case studies show instances in which change is instituted by participants in the incumbent market once it is shown that the change is warranted and has support. This in turn underlines the importance of initiatives by government.

The high cost of being the first supplier of a product is mentioned frequently. Another important category involves barriers relating to insufficient information and problems on the part of customers and users in processing information. This results in high transaction costs that hinder market penetration. The measures prescribed are mostly of the type intended to clarify and verify technology performance through the use of brochures, labels, illustrative calculations and the like. This type of information is often generic and can provide the basis for a wide range of choices made primarily by users as non-specialists.

Barriers associated with financing purchases of equipment and the risks associated with that are mentioned less frequently. The policy measures used to deal with these barriers involve 'active verification' of the performance of technologies. That is, it involves information services tailored to the needs of the individual customer; for instance, of the sort provided by energy service companies.

Price-distortion and the need to internalise costs or make other adjustments to deal with them are hardly mentioned in the case studies; similarly inappropriate regulations are not viewed as a problem. This does not necessarily mean that these kinds of problems are unimportant to programme designers and managers; it could mean simply that they see little chance of success in dealing with such matters.

R&D as a Policy Tool

In examining the case studies in relation to the R&D+Deployment perspective, we watched for references to the state of development of technologies involved in the programmes reported on, the presence or absence of known solutions to technical barriers and whether or not the use of niche markets was considered.

In regard to the state of development of a technology, most of the case studies deal with technologies that are known and understood, but still not developed to such an extent that the market will pick them up easily. From our knowledge of the learning phenomenon we know that growth in production and sales is necessary to overcome many of the technical problems that remain (e.g., high first costs) and adaptations are necessary to make the technologies available to fit user needs and preferences. The measures needed are demonstration projects, help with organising and financing of learning investments, pilot projects to support market adaptation, etc. There are many references to these issues in the case studies.

There are also quite a few cases that deal with existing technologies that are well proven and already distributed. In these cases the matter of concern is increasing market coverage and the issues discussed relate to developing market support; e.g., training programmes for consultants and service providers.

Addressing the problem of identifying niche markets is essential when technology learning is an objective. This factor was not frequently addressed in the cases and is perhaps a neglected aspect of policy development. On the other hand, it may be that case study authors did not see the need to focus on this point. For instance, in cases in which extensive additional research is required to find out if and how a technology will work, deployment issues will not get as much attention. If they are considered in such cases it is in relation to carefully selected producers and customers who give extensive feedback. In this kind of case the exploitation of niche markets is implicit and need not be explicitly mentioned.

Market Transformation

In searching the case studies for evidence of the market transformation perspective, we watched for references to the kinds of products being supported and the market groups being targeted. Regarding the first dimension, the case studies were categorised according to whether they were concerned with: (1) *new products* being made available; (2) *higher sales* of existing good products; or (3) *lower sales* of bad products. Twelve of the case studies involved references to the launching of new products, ten to expanding sales of existing products and in one case there was reference to an objective of reducing sales. The last case refers to a quality-label programme. In general, one would not expect much mention of an objective to reduce sales of an undesirable product because it is usually implicit in the support of a new or existing product.

In the discussion of diffusion curves in Chapter 6 various categories of buyer groups to be targeted were introduced. We identified activities in the case study programmes that could be assigned to these categories (this is admittedly an aspect of the analysis that involves rough judgements). Nine case studies referred to targeting customer groups who are *Innovators*, eleven to *Early Adopters*, twelve to the *Early Majority* – people who are pragmatic but want to avoid risk, three to *Late Majority* customers and one to *Laggards*.

Most of the deployment projects try to reach groups that are likely to lead the market; i.e., buyers who will be imitated by others. By definition this is likely to be a small part of the market and in order to get further it is necessary to reach the two majority categories. Many projects involved attempts to 'cross the chasm' between the Early

Adopters and the Early Majority, which is often the most difficult stage of transforming a market.

Most programmes focus on a small portion of a market in the hope of starting a process that will be self-supporting; thus the category of policy measures that target niche markets is important. Only one programme reported on went so far as to address the totality of a market. It is the quality-label programme mentioned above, which is mandatory. It involves a requirement that for most people does not require immediate action (since it comes in to effect only when a building is sold). Given that mandatory requirements do not easily gain public acceptance, this is an interesting characteristic. Other forms of mandatory requirements are available as policy tools (e.g., building codes).

A Simple Proposal for a More Comprehensive Perspective

Since we have argued that market development policy measures differ across perspectives, it is possible that measures designed in relation to any one perspective will not adequately account for what needs to be done to achieve overall programme objectives. In this light it is useful to think about policy measures as they would come out of a more comprehensive perspective. Our proposal is a simple one: first, step back from the complexity of the specific policy measures themselves and identify the operational objectives that need to be achieved if a market for a new technology is to be developed; then for each operational objective, identify the kind of situation in which it will play a role and list the kinds of measures that might be used to achieve it, taking care to be open to all possibilities and being sensitive to different ways of thinking.

This can be simply an intuitive approach, assuming that the people who are building up the list of objectives and measures are knowledgeable about deployment programmes and their evolution;

and that they are capable of stepping back from their experience and looking at it in a thoughtful way. Or it can be a conscious effort to meld together the distinctive aspects of the three policy perspectives we have discussed – in effect a kind of meta-analysis. In preparing this book we have been trying to engage in that kind of thinking. We have been aided by the perspective-based analysis of the case studies summarised in the preceding section. That is, we decomposed the deployment programmes studied into all of the individual policy measures taken and, to the extent possible, categorised these measures according to which of three perspectives they reflected. We found that many of the measures can be understood in terms of more than one of the three models and, even where they are different, they interact. Thus we realised that policy measures could be repackaged in a more pragmatic way into those needed to achieve 'operational objectives'. We carried out that exercise and the results are shown in Table 7.2.

At the left of Table 7.2 are eight operational objectives that are involved in technology market development programmes. At the right of each objective are some notes that suggest the kind of situation in which that operational objective would be important. The objectives can be organised into three groups, shown at the right of the table:

- *Customer relations* may need attention, meaning that the customer needs to be better served in making choices, presented with price and other incentives that will lead to clever choices, or perhaps needs to be protected from making risky choices.

- *Business and market organisation* may need adjustment. The potential demand from the public for the services of better energy technologies may have to be made manifest to business interests and the supply structure may need vitalisation.

- *Rules and institutions* governing market behaviour may have to be adjusted to allow competition to function better, to avoid favouring or disfavouring alternative technologies for extraneous reasons, or to facilitate better optimisation of an overall energy system.

Table 7.2. Operational Objectives in Deployment Programmes and their Characteristic Applications

Type	Operational Objective	Characteristic Application and Examples of Measures	
A	Serve the customer	The customer/user is assumed to need assistance in making better choices from among available technologies. Some relevant measures: the provision of customer-oriented information and calculation tools; and occasionally some interventions to enhance market functions, e.g., third-party financing, development of energy service companies (ESCOs), etc.	CUSTOMER RELATIONS
B	Incentives for the customer	Good technologies known to customers are not widely adopted because of market imperfections and externalities. Some relevant measures: internalise external costs through tax measures, adjust market structure so that those who benefit from energy efficiency can influence technology choice.	
C	Educate and protect the customer	Inferior technologies are overly used because of inertia on the part of both suppliers and consumers, which weakens competition from new alternatives. E.g., purchasing rules may favour low initial investments and under-estimate high operating costs.	
D	Manifest the demand for a change	Find niche and develop niche markets in which to launch and adapt technologies; their development could start a process of more widespread market uptake. Some relevant measures: work with stakeholders to aggregate product demand; help to finance learning investment.	BUSINESS ORGANISATION
E	Vitalise conservative business structure	The market has got stuck with traditional products delivered in forms that are not always favourable for customers and users. Activities to improve competition (e.g., deregulation) can vitalise market actors.	
F	Reconsider existing regulations and rules	Wider application of good technologies can be hampered by legislation and regulations primarily adapted to conventional technologies. E.g., liberalise regulations affecting electricity feeds from small scale combined production of heat and power (CHP) and independent power producers.	MARKET RULES & INSTITUTIONS
G	Enhance financial framework & conditions	Financial arrangements available to buyers may not be well adjusted to the needs of new energy technology markets and this may impede capital stock turnover and slow the adoption of new technologies. Enhancement of financial conditions may open new opportunities.	
H	Recognise system aspects	A technological solution designed for a specific problem can affect the output of a larger system. Recognition of the totality of the system (energy, comfort, productivity, environment, etc.) is sometimes necessary to understand and handle the technology shift. A typical instrument is the ISO 9000 and 14000 standards.	

Table 7.3 maps the operational objectives of Table 7.2 back into the conceptual categories contained in each of our three policy perspectives (though in developing these ideas the reasoning was to some extent in the opposite direction; i.e., the combination of ideas from the different perspectives led to the definition of the operational policy objectives). This suggests the kind of specific policy actions that could be taken to achieve the operational objectives. For example, for operational objective B – providing appropriate incentive structures for customers of energy technologies – the range of policy measures used to deal with two of the standard market barriers can be brought into play (those having to do with market price distortions and with decision making by people other than those who will benefit from the technology, as in the landlord/tenant problem), as can the financing of technical adaptations for better market coverage and the various market transformation measures for niche markets.

This approach can be extended to build up more comprehensive and detailed packages of individual policy actions that could be used to achieve each operational objective considered. In this short chapter it is not possible to do that, but one can see that this kind of thinking could proceed towards some sort of detailed 'handbook' that would provide the basis for a more holistic approach to deployment policy development, as well as aiding the analysis of deployment programmes that have already been undertaken, of the sort we are doing in this book. Developing such a handbook – in effect, developing a 'How to ...' manual for deployment policy, would clearly be a large project of its own.

It is acknowledged that if an analytical exercise of this sort is pursued in depth it cannot be entirely independent of context – the world is not that simple. For example, on a practical level the list of operational objectives and relevant policy measures that define our analytical framework could depend to some extent on the types and stages of the technologies for which markets are being developed and on national particularities. Doing the exercise for a new type of nuclear reactor will differ from doing it for a new type of light bulb. Nevertheless it is possible to be quite general, as we have illustrated in this discussion.

Table 7.3: Operational Objectives Related to Perspective-Linked Issues

For each operational objective shown in the left-hand column, the Xs in the matrix for that row indicate the aspects of the three perspectives that are relevant. Reading a row of the matrix tells you how the corresponding package of measures would combine ideas from the different perspectives. Reading a column of the matrix tells you the different operational objectives needed to deal with the issue concerned.

Operational objective / Types of Measures	Information — Clarifying technical performance	Transaction cost	Risk — Active verification	Finance	Price Distortion — Correct prices	Market Org – Split incentives — Adapt incentive structure	Market Org – Bias — Adapt market routines	Market Org – cost — Adapt production	Market Org – tradition — Adapt organisation	Regulation — Adapt rules	Capital stock turnover — Timing measures	Tech-specific barrier — Focus technology to market	Existing technology — Expand market coverage	Few Known solutions — Finance market adaptation	Not known solutions — Finance tech development	Niche Market addressed — Identify niche, negotiate	New product — Target niches	More good product — Enable customers	Less bad product — Warn customers
Barrier type described in case study													**Technology R&D+D Target**				**MT Purpose**		
A Serve	X	X	X	X									X				X		
B Incentivise						X	X						X		X	X			
C Educate	X						X		X				X						X
D Manifest								X					X		X	X			
E Vitalise									X				X	X			X		
F Reconsider									X				X				X	X	
G Enhance			X	X	X						X		X			X	X		
H Recognise												X	X			X	X	X	X

Further Empirical Analysis

The overall perspective we have proposed provides a framework for analysing deployment policy either as programmes are being constructed, in order to facilitate a more comprehensive approach, or in efforts to understand programmes that have already been undertaken. Many of the observations on national deployment programmes made in this book were formulated as we systematically examined the case studies in the process of constructing the model described above. We also attempted some more ambitious global analysis, which is the subject of this closing section of the chapter.

We were interested in more insight into how the programmes reported on in the case studies relate to the holistic policy framework defined above. We wanted to see the extent to which the combined approach as embodied in our operational policy objectives was used in the 22 national programmes. That is, having postulated a generalised deployment programme framework, we wanted to use it as a hypothetical criterion of comprehensiveness in relation to some actual programmes.

We thus went through each case study to infer from it the measures that were diagnosed as necessary to achieve programme objectives, identify the actual measures instituted, and record the results of the programme as reported in the case studies. (The result of this data-development effort is briefly summarised on a case-by-case basis in the Appendix to this book.) For each case study we made a judgement on how the policy measures undertaken could be categorised into packages associated with the eight generalised operational objectives defined in Table 7.2. We then made a second judgement as to whether each package of measures was actually applied. The results were tabulated, summarised and examined in search of patterns.

We have not reported these numerical results here for various reasons having to do with the problems involved in this sort of data analysis. Working up the data for such an analysis involves a considerable amount of subjective judgement. This can be dealt with by way of cross-checking the judgements of several analysts, which is a time-consuming process that was not feasible as part of the preparation of this book and not really warranted in light of the nature of these case studies. The latter point is true because the case-study template was not designed with these sorts of questions in mind. If one wanted to pursue this line of data analysis diligently it would be desirable to do a new sample survey that would include questions defined specifically in relation to our new analytical framework. This would also get around the problem of circular reasoning involved in first designing the criterion of comprehensiveness on the basis of this set of case studies and then using it to evaluate the same set of projects according to that criterion.

All that notwithstanding, it is worthwhile noting some of the results of the exercise very briefly in order to illustrate the kinds of issues that can be considered in this framework and because they are also interesting merely as an additional way of summarising some of the information in this set of case studies. For instance, the following observations indicate which of the operational objectives defined in Table 7.2 were frequently applied in these 22 projects and which were not.

■ In the area of *Customer Relations,* the most frequently applied measures and the best fit of measures to the diagnosis of what was needed is for package A, measures intended to serve the customer, whereas incentive packages (objective B) or educating and protecting the consumer (C) were either less used or less well targeted in the early stages of the programmes. That is, the latter two categories more often involved change and reconfiguration.

■ In the area of *Business Organisation,* measures designed to make demand potential manifest (objective D) were more often applied and well targeted than measures aimed at vitalising business (E). The latter were in some cases not targeted in the diagnosis but later instituted.

■ In the area of setting *Rules and Market Conditions,* these needs were seldom noted at the diagnosis stage. In the case of the need to reconsider regulations (package F), this perhaps reflects that the current interest in regulatory reform is relatively new in relation to the start-dates for many of the programmes. Enhancement of the market framework (G) was also relatively little alluded to as an objective, perhaps for a similar reason, though it also should be noted that the policy instruments in this area are not usually in the hands of the energy policy makers and one should therefore not be surprised that this issue was not considered. The most frequently applied types of measure in this area are those that recognise system dependency (H). It also seems that this area more often involves trial-and-error correction than the other two.

Finally the results made it appear that in the planning and definition phase, programme managers often did not fully recognise the problems that needed to be solved, but that as information on implementation was fed back to them, project design and application was improved. For a variety of reasons, during the implementation of a programme some measures may be dropped or changed. This is hardly surprising, especially for programmes that run over a long time period. In fact, the results of the change of plans may be very positive. The changes may often be highly warranted and the outcome excellent – an illustration of the learning process that we believe to be so important. Alternatively, the changes could reflect a lack of funds, mismanagement or a change of direction in regard to government objectives.

CHAPTER 8: CONCLUSIONS
WHAT HAVE WE LEARNED?

The scope for benefits to society from the deployment of cleaner and more efficient energy technologies is very great. Some of the potential for applying new technologies is not realised or is delayed because of inertia in the markets for established technologies and because so many potential buyers are not aware of the benefits available or do not find them large enough to warrant the effort involved in pursuing them actively. Yet the aggregate volume of benefits – those enjoyed directly by the buyer, combined with the benefits of a healthier environment for everyone – may be well worth the effort for society as a whole. Hence the subject of this book: what can we learn about the nature of success in technology deployment policy?

Our contention at the outset was that policy development in this area has been influenced by three overlapping perspectives. We learned in separate chapters that each of those perspectives provides a rich framework for interpreting the experience with technology deployment programmes reported on in the 22 case studies submitted to the IEA. While they overlap, each perspective emphasises different issues and has a different overall tone. The R&D+Deployment perspective focuses on the technical knowledge base and its interactions with deployment. It provides a rationale for learning investments and a future-oriented outlook. The market barriers perspective, grounded in economic theory, provides criteria for market efficiency and discipline in regard to the nature and extent of government interventions in the market-place. The market transformation perspective focuses on the practice of technology deployment, building upon the insights and techniques of the private sector and transferring this approach to the design and implementation of public policy. However, any one of the perspectives in isolation is insufficient. For example, the R&D+Deployment approach places a value on organisational learning, but transferring the understanding of that phenomenon into government policy requires inputs from the other two approaches. Similarly the economists' tools lucidly expose important issues involved in decision-making, but their abstract nature limits their scope; dependence on them can lead analysts to overlook practical problems and dynamic processes associated with the emergence of markets for new technologies. The other two perspectives help to fill in those gaps.

Fortunately many people involved in deployment policy develop a personal perspective on their work that embodies components of all three approaches. This is something to be encouraged. The most important overall lesson learned from examining the IEA case studies is that policy-making should be approached in a comprehensive way, a way that accounts for all aspects of the innovation process. In our view, a synthesis of the R&D+Deployment, market barriers and market transformation perspectives will go a long way to achieving that goal.

We have attempted to apply this approach to analysing the case studies. In Chapter 6 we drew ideas pragmatically from the three perspectives in a discussion of analytical tools and the question of how to evaluate success in a broad context. In a more formal attempt at synthesis in Chapter 7, we described how we attempted a 'triangulation' analysis of the case studies. This involved unbundling the facts of each study and categorising them in terms of their relation to the three perspectives. This helped us to define a series of operational objectives that can be used as stepping-stones to developing packages of policy measures that draw ideas from all three policy perspectives as appropriate. Thus our analysis of the case studies led us to propose a more holistic framework for formulating deployment initiatives. We believe that its use would result in a more integrated approach to programme design and implementation. A first step in an effort to apply these ideas could be the development of a manual for deployment programmes based on the framework sketched out in Chapter 7.

Describing the more detailed kinds of insights we got from a close reading of the case studies is difficult, given the diversity and complexity of the technologies, markets and measures covered. The summary observations below convey some of the most important lessons we perceived:

■ A necessary starting point for the development of deployment measures is a recognition of the interests of all of the stakeholders in a market for an energy technology.

■ Effort is needed to mobilise those interests in the pursuit of improved performance, lower costs and wider dissemination of the technology involved. The reshaping and the invigoration of interactions among stakeholders can make a major contribution to success. Interaction can be improved by removing or reducing barriers that impede market activity, facilitating communication between R&D providers and equipment suppliers, taking better account of the nature of buyer- and user-attitudes, and in many other ways.

■ The various measures that make up a technology deployment programme must be coherent and harmonised among themselves and with policies for industrial development, environmental control, taxation and other areas of government activity that affect market conditions for the technology.

■ Feedback mechanisms among market actors need to be well-developed and active. They can help suppliers to use R&D resources more productively and both producers and consumers to learn by doing.

■ Similarly deployment programmes themselves are more likely to succeed when they involve monitoring that leads to feedback and trouble-shooting. Many of the national programmes studied were adjusted as they proceeded because managers became aware of problems in programme design and complexities in the targeted markets that had not been accounted for.

■ There is much potential for saving energy hidden in small-scale purchases: the gathering and focusing of purchasing power is an important opportunity for the deployment of new, cleaner energy technologies.

■ Most consumers have little interest in energy issues *per se*, but would gladly respond to energy efficiency measures or use renewable fuels as part of a package with features they do care about.

In the end it is the combined effect of technology performance and customer acceptance that make an impact on the market and hence on energy systems. Developing a deeper understanding of both, including how they are influenced by the actions of government, is an essential ingredient of effective deployment policy.

In closing we should remind ourselves why all of this matters. Why, after all, should we care enough to try to design effective, ambitious and successful deployment programmes for efficient and clean energy technologies? The answer is that we need to have new energy technologies in the market to respond to some of the grand challenges of our day – most notably the problems of climate change and other environmental impacts of energy use, but also the consequences for economic security of our continuing, even rising, dependence on fossil fuels. We need to release the potential that already exists because better technology is available but is not widely adopted. And we need to build additional potential by supporting the development and deployment of promising new energy technologies. We have discussed the importance of learning processes in this book. Realising these potentials through effective policy-making requires a commitment to learning in its broadest, most integrated and positive sense – the capacity to recognise the economic, environmental and societal challenges around us, and the willingness to respond to them with equal doses of responsibility and ingenuity.

SOURCES USED

Abell, D.F. and Hammond, J.S. (1979) "Cost Dynamics: Scale and Experience Effects", in: *Strategic Planning: Problems and Analytical Approaches*, Prentice Hall, Englewood Cliffs, N.J.

Argyris, C. and Schön, D.A. (1978) *Organizational Learning: A Theory of Action Perspective*, Addison-Wesley, Reading MA.

Blumstein, Carl, Seymour Goldstone & Loren Lutzenhiser (1998) "A Theory-based Approach to Market Transformation", paper presented to the *Summer Study on Energy Efficiency In Buildings*, American Council for an Energy Efficient Economy (ACEEE), Washington, DC.

Boston Consulting Group (1968) *Perspectives on experience*, Boston Consulting Group Inc.

Durstewitz, M. and M. Hoppe-Kilpper (1999) "Using information of Germany's "250 MW Wind"-Programme for the Construction of Wind Power Experience Curves", in C.-O. Wene, A. Voss, T. Fried (Eds.) *Proceedings, IEA Workshop on Experience Curves for Policy Making – The Case of Energy Technologies*, p. 129, 10-11 May 1999, Stuttgart, Germany, Forschungsbericht 67, Institut für Energiewirtschaft und Rationelle Energieanwendung, Universität Stuttgart.

Espejo, R., Schuhmann,W., Schwaninger, M. and Bilello, U. (1996) *Organizational Transformation and Learning – A Cybernetic Approach to Management*, John Wiley & Sons Ltd, Chichester.

EU-SAVE (2000) "Monitoring of energy efficiency trends for refrigerators, freezers, washing machines and washer-dryers sold in the EU". SAVE contract N. XVII/4.1031/Z/98-251, Final Report.

Geller, Howard & Steven Nadel (1994) "Market Transformation Strategies to Promote End-use Efficiency", *Annual Review of Energy and the Environment*, 19:301-346.

Harmon, C. (2000) "Experience Curves of Photovoltaic Technology", *IIASA Interim Report IR-00-014*, International Institute for Applied Systems Analysis, Laxenburg, Austria.

Hirst, E. & M. Brown (1991) "Closing the efficiency gap: Barriers to the efficient use of energy" *Resources, Conservation, and Recycling*, 3, 267-281.

Horowitz, Marvin J. (2001) "Economic Indicators of Market Transformation: Energy Efficient Lighting and EPA's Green Lights", *The Energy Journal*, Vol. 22, No. 4.

International Association of Energy Efficient Lighting (2000) "Soaring CFL sales", *IAEEL Newsletter* 1-2.

Iwafune, Y. (2000) "Technology Progress Dynamics of Compact Fluorescent Lamps", *IIASA Interim Report IR-00-009*, IIASA Laxenburg, Austria.

Kemp, R. (1997), *Environmental Policy and Technical Change*, Cheltenham, Edward Elgar.

Kemp, R. et al (1998) "Regime shifts to sustainability through process of niche formation: the approach of strategic niche management", *Technology Analysis and Strategy Management*, 10, 175-195.

Kliman, Mel (2001) "Developing markets for new energy technologies: A review of the case studies from the market barrier perspective", Paper presented to IEA Workshop, *Technologies Require Markets: Best Practices and Lessons Learned in Energy Technology Deployment Policies*, Paris, 28-29 November. (Available on the attached CD-ROM).

Kopp, Raymond J., Alan J. Krupnick and Michael Toman (1997) *Cost-Benefit Analysis and Regulatory Reform: An Assessment of the Science and the Art*, Resources for the Future, Washington, DC; Discussion Paper 97-19. (Available at http://www.rff.org/proj_summaries/files/kopp_bencost_primer.htm.)

Kunkle, Rick & Loren Lutzenhiser (1998) "The Evolution of Market Transformation", *Proceedings of the ACEEE Summer Study on Energy Efficiency In Buildings*, Washington, DC, USA.

Lund, Peter (2001) "Market Transformation Perspective and Involvement of Market Actors and Stakeholders in the IEA Case Studies", Paper presented to IEA Workshop, *Technologies Require Markets: Best Practices and Lessons Learned in Energy Technology Deployment Policies*, Paris, 28-29 November. (Available on the attached CD-ROM)

Moore, G.A. (1991) *Crossing the chasm: Marketing and selling technology Products to Mainstream Customers*, HCP, New York.

Morgan, G. (1986), *Images of Organization*, Sage Publications, Newbury Park.

Neij, Lena (1999) "Cost dynamics of wind power", *Energy*, Vol 24, p. 375.

—— (1999) *Dynamics of Energy Systems. Methods of analysing Technology Change*, Lund University.

Nilsson, H. (1996) "Looking inside the box of market transformation", *Proceedings of ACEEE Summer Study on Energy Efficiency in Buildings*, Asilomar, California, August, 1996, p.5.181.

Nilsson, H. and Wene, C.-O. (2002) "Best Practices in Technology Deployment Policies", *Proceedings of ACEEE Summer Study on Energy Efficiency in Buildings*, Asilomar, California, 18-23 August, 2002, p. 9.267.

OECD/IEA (1997a) *Enhancing the Market Deployment of Energy Technology – A Survey of Eight Technologies*, Paris.

—— (1997b) *Energy Efficiency Initiative*, Volume 1, Paris.

—— (2000) *Experience Curves for Energy Technology Policy*, Paris.

—— (2001) *Energy Labels & Standards*, Paris.

Palmer, Jane and Brenda Boardman (1998), *DELight, Domestic Efficient Lighting*, Energy and Environment Change Unit, University of Oxford.

Reddy, A.K.N. (1991) "Barriers to improvement in energy efficiency", *Energy Policy*, 19(7):953-61.

Rogers, E.M. (1995) *Diffusion of Innovations*, Free Press, New York.

Schrattenholzer, Leo (2001) "Analyzing the Case Studies from the Perspective of the R&D and Deployment Model", Paper presented to IEA Workshop, *Technologies Require Markets: Best Practices and Lessons Learned in Energy Technology Deployment Policies*, Paris, 28-29 November. (Available on the attached CD-ROM)

Sutherland, Ronald J. (1991). "Market Barriers to Energy-Efficiency Investments", *The Energy Journal*, (12)3.

Tatutani, Marika (1995) "Market Transformation in Action: A Report from the Consortium for Energy Efficiency", *Energy Services Journal*, 1:109-118.

USDOE (2001) *Pump Life Cycle Costs: A Guide to LCC Analysis for Pumping Systems*, Executive Summary, Office of Industrial Technology, Washington. Available at http://www.oit.doe.gov/bestpractices/technical_publications.shtml#bp.

Watanabe, C. (1995) "Identification of the Role of Renewable Energy – A View from Japan's Challenge: The New Sunshine Program", *Renewable Energy*, Vol. 6, p. 237.

—— (1999) "Industrial Dynamism and the Creation of a "Virtuous Cycle" between R&D, Market Growth and Price Reduction – The Case of Photovoltaic Power Generation (PV) Development in Japan", in C.-O. Wene, A. Voss, T. Fried (Eds.) *Proceedings, IEA Workshop on Experience Curves for Policy Making – The Case of Energy Technologies*, p. 7, 10-11 May 1999, Stuttgart, Germany, Forschungsbericht 67, Institut für Energiewirtschaft und Rationelle Energieanwendung, Universität Stuttgart.

Wene, C.-O. (1999) "Experience Curves: Measuring the Performance of the Black Box", in C.-O. Wene, A. Voss, T. Fried (Eds.) *Proceedings IEA Workshop on Experience Curves for Policy Making – The Case of Energy Technologies*, p. 53, 10-11 May 1999, Stuttgart, Germany, Forschungsbericht 67, Institut für Energiewirtschaft und Rationelle Energieanwendung, Universität Stuttgart.

Westling, Hans (2000) *Final Management Report – Task III*, IEA DSM Implementing Agreement. (Available at http://dsm.iea.org.)

ANNEX: CASE DIAGNOSES, MEASURES AND RESULTS

This Annex summarises the data developed for the analysis described in the last section of Chapter 7. In addition to providing the reader with more insight into the nature of that analysis, the 22 sections below also provide some summary information on the results of the programmes reported on in the case studies.

The following headings were used for categorising the information in the box for each case study:

- **Diagnosis of measures needed** – From our reading of the case studies we inferred the diagnosis of the problems to be solved and the measures to be taken as made by the programme designers and related them to the 'operational objectives' defined in Table 7.2.

- **Match of measures to policies** – We identified the measures actually instituted as part of the programme and related them to the operational objectives as defined in Table 7.2. This provided a framework within which to focus on the effectiveness of programme design and on the evolution of the programme as it developed over time (including the possibility of changes in the diagnosis of what was needed).

- **Volume growth** – Reported growth in sales of the technology concerned or related variables.

- **Volume and market penetration** – In some cases additional quantitative information was reported on the market impact of the deployment programme.

- **Volume and price/cost** – If quantitative information on learning effects was included in the case study it is reported under this heading.

- **Attribution of impacts to measures** – Information in the case studies that had a bearing on evaluating the success of measures taken is reported under this heading.

- **Performance improvement** – Quantitative measures provided in the case studies that compare the performance of the technology covered by the programme to the conventional technologies favoured in the market.

- **Programme cost** – Overall costs of the programme.

- **Estimated savings of energy or related variables due to programme** – In a few cases estimates of this sort were available.

- **Remarks** – Each section concludes with some very brief comments about distinctive aspects of the deployment programme concerned and its success.

Where any one of these headings does not appear in a section, the relevant summary information was not provided in the case study.

Note that information on programme impacts in the sections below comes only from the case studies, which were typically based on information available in 2000. While the impacts of many of these programmes have increased since that time, the data used in this Annex have not been updated.

1. Deployment of Biomass District Heating (BMDH), Austria

Started 1980. By 1999 more than 500 small-scale plants have been established.

Diagnosis of measures needed: The programme focuses on the service needed to have customers accept and use a basically known technology, though one not being applied in this small-size range or in the target area; and on the need to vitalise the market and those involved in it by giving them a helping hand and a concept that can be shown to work.

Match of measures to policies: The measures are according to the diagnosis, though there seems to have been a development towards several related issues, the most dominant of which fall under operational objective D of Table 7.2 (manifesting a demand for change) – to focus business interest, assure sufficient financing and above all to place the project in an overall context of seeking coherent approaches to agricultural and regional development.

Results:

- Volume growth: Up to 1999 more than 500 BMDH units established in rural areas serving 500-4 000 inhabitants. Of these 2/3 are of a size less than 1 500 kW.

- Volume and market penetration: Dissemination has grown steadily over the years up to approximately 30 sites per year. Since mid-1990 plants of less than 800 kW have become more important, whereas bigger ones are held back. These plants provide about 10% of the total heat from biofuel in Austria, which is 17% of the total Austrian heat demand.

- Volume and price/cost: There are indications that improvements have been made by the use of 'niche managers' to advise on technologies and economy.

- Performance improvement: Not known, though trouble-shooting by the niche managers likely means some improvement and standardisation.

- Programme cost: Some costs for regional development and agricultural support have to be included. The total programme required some 25 MEuro up to 1999. The subsidy could be as high as 50% of the investment.

Remarks: This is a highly innovative programme. Feedback from programme experience has led to programme adjustments, as has the identification of new groups. Policy coherence has been an objective.

2. Thermoprofit (Part of the Graz Municipal Energy Concept), Austria

Thermoprofit is a trademark for total service packages to reduce the amount of energy consumed in a building. The project certifies ESCOs as partners and uses third-party financing and performance contracting as a model.

Diagnosis of measures needed: Primarily a service package (operational objective A) to customers who have limited capacity to handle an energy efficiency project or in some cases (e.g., municipal institutions) to finance them. Also in the diagnostic framework are customer protective elements and elements aimed at reconsidering rules for this type of project.

Match of measures to policies: The measures taken accord with the diagnostics, except that the element to vitalise business seems to have grown stronger in actual applications.

Results: (Reported results are limited, since the programme began less than 2 years before the case study was written.)

■ Volume growth: Several Projects have been identified.

■ Volume and market penetration: Certification of 5 companies in October 1999.

Remark: Provides security for the customer by way of the authorisation of ESCOs and by transparent, standardised, certified methods for project handling; this is especially important for users with little own resources. The model has interesting characteristics since the role and development of ESCOs are often discussed.

3. Renewable Energy Deployment Initiative (REDI), Canada

Launched on April 1, 1998 as a 3-year programme that has been extended for 3 more years until March 31, 2004.

Diagnosis of measures needed: The diagnosis seems oriented to the reshaping of the market by vitalising business, aggregating demand and giving customers incentives to act.

Match of measures to policies: The measures go in the same direction as the diagnosis by manifesting demand, but the programme is wider and more general in the choice of measures used. The change pursued is tailored to have a lasting effect on several groups in the chain of goods and service delivered to customers.

Results:

- Programme cost: 8 million US$ over a 3-year period
- Attribution of impacts to measures: Indicated but unclear

Remark: The programme has an interesting architecture, which addresses several important issues, but at the time the case study was prepared it was too early to report on results. There is a sense in the diagnosis that an overall market transformation is being pursued; it would be useful to track the achievements of market participants in this programme and proceed from there.

4. Mandatory Energy Labelling of Buildings in Denmark

Developed in the context of a long history of energy auditing activities, including the Heat Consultant Scheme, which was in effect from 1982 to 1996. The development of energy labelling was needed to improve and modernise this scheme.

Diagnosis of measures needed: The description of the rationale for the programme strongly emphasises service for customers.

Match of measures to policies: The measures are consistent with the service objective but also apply strongly to operational objective C (protecting the customer, in the sense of giving them the means to understand calculations that could be biased, for example, by the choice of parameters for the lifetime of equipment and of the sources of advice) and to objective F, reconsidering the rules that guide market activities, such as the information that must be available in a purchasing situation.

Results:

■ Volume growth: 40-50 000 labellings per year

■ Volume and market penetration: 160 000 labellings (10% of market) reached in 3.5 years

■ Volume and price/cost: 300-500 Euro per labelling

■ Attribution of impacts to measures: 26% of households have implemented measures and 22% state their intention to do so in a near future

■ Performance improvement: An average household could lower their energy bill by 20%

■ Programme cost: 750 000 Euro per year (refers to programme development paid by the Danish Energy Agency)

■ Estimated savings of energy or related variables due to programme: Savings of 130 000 MEuro have been identified (20 MEuro per annum if implemented)

Remark: This is an important programme that works by taking account of the interests of market actors and has been adapted in response to feedback from those affected. This mandatory scheme has addressed areas that are complicated and tough to deal with, in that it applies to existing buildings and its target population includes customers who have little interest and/or perception of the problem. The programme is in a form that will provide accumulated results over time, in that people implement measures when it fits into their own plans.

5. Diesel Engines for Combined Cycle Power Generation, Finland

Diagnosis of measures needed: Strong focus on operational objective H to find the correct function of a technology in relation to a larger system, making the best use of available knowledge and manufacturing capability. The case study also conveys a strong interest in industrial development.

Match of measures to policies: The measures fit the diagnosis very well. The partners use financial mechanisms and tax instruments that enable the participation aimed for.

Results:

- Volume and market penetration: The demonstration has reached a large number of important target groups (9 000 visits from 4 500 possible investors)

- Attribution of impacts to measures: Direct responses observed and incentives (tax reductions) are well tailored for users

Remark: This project focuses on product development and demonstration that involves many stakeholders and uses their experience and interest actively. The relation of the case study to deployment issues is not strong because the target is set in terms of technology and not in market terms. It could be viewed as a project that precedes deployment programmes and in that sense involves interesting promise.

6. Solar Optimised Buildings, 'SolarBau'. Energy Efficiency and Solar Energy Use in the Commercial Building Sector, Germany

Diagnosis of measures needed: The diagnosis seems weak and split between objectives; it primarily acknowledges that demand is weak and ought to be strengthened, and that financing is a problem.

Match of measures to policies: The measures are primarily geared towards financing R&D associated with technology-specific issues as they are related to the systems function. Thus there is little coherence with the diagnosis made.

Results:

- Attribution of impacts to measures: Knowledge development among important categories of skill needed in the work (that of architects, engineers, etc.) and about critical pieces of system configuration seem well addressed.

- Performance improvement: The case study indicates that objectives have been reached (total energy demand <100 kWh/m^2a and space heating <40 kWh/m^2a). It reports that the result so far is well above expectations and points to a reduction of energy use in targeted commercial buildings, which is down to 1/5 of present average value.

Remark: The project reported on in the case study is not focused on deployment issues, it deals primarily with systems technology for a small group that want to test and demonstrate a capacity to design in a pilot scale.

7. Wind Power for Grid Connection '250 MW Wind' Programme, Germany

Started in 1989, the closing date is scheduled for 2006. Initially started as the '100 MW Wind' programme; because of a high level of demand, and the reunification of Germany, funding was expanded to a total of 250 MW in 1991.

Diagnosis of measures needed: The case study description is not very precise in terms of diagnosing targets; it gives the impression that financing or cost barriers prevent wider use of and future deployment of wind power.

Match of measures to policies: The measures applied are more distinct; it is clear that the programme sets out to improve incentives for the customer and make manifest the demand for wind development. A bit less clear, but nevertheless observable, is that the measures are directed to adjustments in the financing framework, at least in the context of this particular programme.

Results:

■ Volume growth: Total wind power capacity in Germany > 5 000 MW, with 10 TWh/y production

■ Volume and market penetration: Local markets (e.g. Schleswig-Holstein) are supplied up to 15% by wind power (the goal for 2010 is 25%)

■ Volume and price/cost: German manufactured turbines have increased to 10% of world market and have created 15 000 jobs. Specific Investment is appr. 900 Euro/kW

■ Performance improvement: Availability of turbines > 98%, output 2 000 kWh/kW

■ Programme cost: 160 MEuro + 25 MEuro (for monitoring) until 2006

Remark: The programme involves a combination of incentives and other elements that are directed towards one common goal – providing incentives for output and harmonising stakeholders actions. There are also positive effects on employment.

8. Photovoltaic Power Generation Systems (from R&D to Deployment), Japan

Initially started in 1974 as a part of the 'Sunshine Project'.

Diagnosis of measures needed: There is a distinct focus on the aggregation of demand to build a market and on the development of the product involved, both in terms of the nature of the product itself and its role as a system element.

Match of measures to policies: The application of measures seems to be a bit broader than the diagnosis; it stresses both customer and business perspectives. The close connection between the R&D programme and the deployment programme underpins and reinforces the aim to make products more available by development.

Results:

- Volume growth: 200 MW has been installed by end of 1999. Between 1994 and 1999 17000 installations have been made.

- Volume and price/cost: Cost dropped from 30 000 US$/kW (1993) to 8 000 US$/kW (1999)

- Attribution of impacts to measures: Overall impacts are evident, though the blend of measures prevents detailed analysis of each component.

- Performance improvement: As an example, integrated PV modules have been standardised and made part of accepted applications in building codes.

- Programme cost: Many components of the R&D and deployment budgets are tightly fitted and tuned together. Subsidies to customers are in the area of 20% (0.18 MY/kW of 0.93 MY/kW) of installation (1999).

Remark: The range of involvement and the balancing of resources and interests are impressive.

9. High Efficiency Heat Recovery for Domestic Ventilation in the Netherlands.

Mechanical Ventilation with Heat Recovery

Diagnosis of measures needed: The diagnosis indicates that the technology is known but not sufficiently applied according to its merits.

Hence customers and business need to be mobilised, with voluntary participation but supported by rules that facilitate solutions.

Match of measures to policies: The measures are in total harmony with the diagnosis, though the vitalisation of business indicated in the diagnosis, which required price guarantees and certification of installers, was not accepted by the suppliers.

Results:

- Volume growth: 8500 units in new houses (1999).

- Volume and market penetration: grew from 1% installation in houses built during a year (1995) to 10% (1999). The projection for year 2000 is 15%.

- Performance improvement: From 65% energy efficiency on average in normal exchangers to 90-95%. The energy use in fans separately dropped by 40% (shift from AC fans to DC fans). Also indoor air quality, thermal comfort and noise levels have improved.

- Programme cost: 200 000 Euro annually

Remark: This programme involves the use of regulatory instruments and technology development in a comprehensive strategy addressing several issues of importance for both users and suppliers.

10. The PV-Covenant in the Netherlands

Diagnosis of measures needed: According to the diagnosis the customer is the force that should drive the process of change by incentives and the aggregation of demand. The need to reach new customer groups, whose interest is not primarily technology but comfort, is addressed

Match of measures to policies: The measures also emphasise the customer role as the driving force and the use of financial and fiscal instruments to achieve the results. The involvement of several links in the business chain is recognised and used.

Results:

- Volume growth: Goal of 7.7 MW grid-connected solar-PV before year 2000 was reached.

- Volume and price/cost: Not known, but probably a high impact, since the goal for 2007 has been raised significantly (250 MW).

- Attribution of impacts to measures: Highly probable, since the utilities are involved and have signed on to commitments within a voluntary agreement.

- Programme cost: Total amount in programme is 60 MUS$, of which 25 MUS$ for R&D, for four years.

Remark: Stakeholders on the supply side were identified and brought together so that each could use his abilities for a common goal.

11. Deployment of Renewable Energy in a Liberalised Energy Market by Fiscal Instruments in the Netherlands

Goals for 2020: a) 33% improvement of efficiency (total energy consumption should remain at the 1990 level despite economic growth); b) 10% of all energy used should be from renewable sources.

Diagnosis of measures needed: Dutch policy in this area involves components from all three of the broad categories of operational objectives; e.g., buyer incentives, vitalising of business and changing market rules.

Match of measures to policies: The measures taken match well with the diagnosis. The evolution of objectives has been influenced by the need to have flexible policies that allow innovations in both technologies and organisation in a setting of deregulated electricity markets.

Results:

- Volume growth: Market has grown from 600 GWh to 1400 GWh in four years

- Volume and market penetration: Green Energy is used by 3.5% of all households and in some customer groups up to 10%.

- Volume and price/cost: Obviously a positive enough result, since competitiveness has been achieved. There is a shortage of contracts in the short term.

- Performance improvement: Not known, but the programme states that the measures used work fine for 'distribution' but that other policy instruments are needed to address the long lead-times in project development.

Remark: This is a comprehensive system for the maximum use of market forces in the achievement of goals by fiscal instruments. It requires careful balancing and consensus among stakeholders.

12. Market Transformation on Lighting, Sweden

Diagnosis of measures needed: The programme aimed primarily at operational objective D – the aggregation of demand for better technology.

Match of measures to policies: The measures came to have a broader range since the aggregation required supportive actions to reach a 'fuzzy' target group and to maintain the aggregated demand. Thus customer service and the development of supplementary market rules and technology systems aspect came into focus.

Results:

- Volume growth: the market grew from 10 000 to 600 000 units/ year in the period 1991-96.

- Volume and market penetration: HF technology is now practically standard when refurbishing is done in the commercial sector

- Volume and price/cost: Life cycle cost for HF-lighting is lower and the prices of ballasts for HF luminaires has dropped

- Attribution of impacts to measures: Highly likely, since installation companies were allies in the programme

- Performance improvement: 10 W per m^2 vs 25 W per m^2. However, improvements in light quality were more important for the user than the energy savings.

- Programme cost: 5.3 MEuro

- Estimates of energy savings and related impacts due to programme: Cost per kWh saved = 0,11 Eurocents

Remark: Based on a technology procurement, supporting activities in this programme were tailored to address the needs for important market stakeholders. Quick market uptake and learning effects were recorded.

13. Market Transformation on Heat pumps, Sweden

Diagnosis of measures needed: The programme aimed primarily at the aggregation of demand for better technology.

Match of measures to policies: In addition to operational objective D, measures taken in the execution of the programme seem also to have covered some aspects of customer protection and more importantly some system-functions and the interdependence between them needed to deliver the final 'energy services' involved.

Results:

- Volume growth: Sales grew from 2 000 units/year (1995) to 11 000 units/year (1997)

- Volume and price/cost: The cost of the initial-purchase package was 30% lower than the corresponding package delivered before the project.

- Attribution of impacts to measures: The market has remained on the newly attained level. According to the manufacturers, the project restored market confidence in heat pumps and led to investments and new jobs in their industry.

- Performance improvement: Equipment performance (COP) was improved by 30%

- Programme cost: 0.5 MUS$

- Programme energy savings: Initially (one year after the programme) 30-40 GWh/year

Remark: This programme acted as a catalyst to start a process that was stuck because suppliers were too small to respond to the challenge and customers were insufficiently informed on the technical aspects of the technology to be able to communicate their needs.

14. EAES Programme, the Swedish Programme for an Environmentally Adapted Energy System

This programme is primarily directed towards projects in the Baltic Region and Eastern Europe (Estonia, Latvia, Lithuania, Poland and Russia).

Diagnosis of measures needed: In the preparations it appears that the focus was on the gaps that were observable in a system of markets in transition. Customers had little information and needed service; the rules related to energy systems and the implementation of energy-related projects were inadequate for a market economy and the systems were improperly configured.

Match of measures to policies: The measures applied were in harmony with the diagnosis, except that they seem to have given more emphasis to the vitalisation of business than to the changing of rules and regulations; that is, the interactions with business under the programme have been more specific than general. The real surprise is that though financing was a primary instrument, in the end it is not an important characteristic of the programme. That is, it seems as if the financing did not need to be restructured, but financial resources had to be made available for projects of a smaller scale.

Results:

■ Volume growth: Significant growth has occurred; the more than 60 projects involved represent some 75% of the entire stock of UN-FCCC registered AIJ-projects (Activities Implemented Jointly) for energy efficiency and renewable fuels.

■ Volume and price/cost: Fuel costs have typically been reduced by 40% by the change from fossil fuel to biofuel.

■ Attribution of impacts to measures: The direct effects can be easily observed.

■ Performance improvement: During a period of some 4-5 years, programme expenditure on consultants dropped from 20% to 10% and the amount of equipment imported from 70% to 35%.

■ Programme cost: 25-30 MUS$

■ Estimates of energy savings and related impacts due to programme: CO_2 reductions of 300 000 tonnes per year, SO_2 3 100 tonnes per year, NO_x 170 tonnes per year. The projects have an estimated life time 15-20 years.

Remark: This programme involves an innovative use of existing knowledge and resources; it addresses important obstacles with many spin-offs.

15. Energy Efficiency Best Practice Programme, UK

Launched in April 1989, to stimulate energy savings in industry, buildings and the business use of transport energy

Diagnosis of measures needed: The programme has been totally focused on serving the customer by providing the information necessary to choose and use technologies at the high-efficiency end of the range of available technologies.

Match of measures to policies: Measures applied are totally consistent with the diagnosis; an element of buyer protection has been added, in that by using the information provided the customer acquires insight into energy-related choices that should be avoided.

Results:

- Attribution of impacts to measures: Evaluations of programme impacts are routinely carried out.

- Programme Cost: Estimated to be 30-45 Euro per tonne of carbon. Funding from the government is in the range of 30 MEuro per year.

- Estimates of energy savings and related impacts due to programme: The programme is expected to save energy according to a ratio of at least 5:1 relative to the programme funding provided. During the period 1989-99 energy savings have been estimated to reach approximately 1 000 MEuro per year, with saving of 4 Mtonnes of carbon per year.

Remark: This case study provides a good example of how a programme can develop over time and accommodate new circumstances. It covers a very wide range of applications and has an exemplary reporting and evaluation system.

16. Unconventional Natural Gas Exploration & Production, United States

Diagnosis of measures needed: The diagnosis focuses on the possible utilisation of a resource that is indicated but not fully known; the assumption is that technology development might demonstrate and facilitate future use of the resource. Programme measures need to be directed at systems utilisation and development.

Match of measures to policies: The measures undertaken show how exploitation of the natural gas resource was made possible by way of a strong financial incentive and a consequently manifest demand from customers who took the risks involved in early adoption of the new technologies. There was also significant backup of the deployment effort by way of R&D.

Results:

- Volume growth: Gas provided from these unconventional sources has grown threefold in 20 years. Growth continued after the programme when tax credits had been phased out. Proven reserves grew about 2.5 times

- Volume and price/cost: There are indications that costs could have been reduced by 50% during the time that tax credits were given

- Attribution of impacts to measures: Highly likely that the programme instigated the development of both technology and knowledge about unconventional gas reserves.

- Performance improvement: Gas has been made available from new reserves.

Remark: This is a combination of an R&D programme in a high risk activity and a system of incentives to attract developers. In regard to the latter aspect there is some resemblance with the Dutch programme reported on in CS11. However, the market concerned is very special and it could be assumed that the number of market actors involved in it is limited and easier to approach for that reason.

17. Sub-Compact Fluorescent Lamps, United States

Diagnosis of measures needed: The target was business organisation and the primary objective to aggregate demand in order to generate interest on the part of manufacturers.

Match of measures to policies: The measures were totally in line with the diagnosis and perhaps even a bit stronger in regard to vitalising business (ensuring that manufacturers saw the possibilities and that customers were communicating their preferences effectively).

Results:

■ Volume growth: The goal of one million lamps was exceeded by 50%.

■ Volume and price/cost: Prevailing prices of 15-22 US$ dropped to the range of 5-8.5 US$ (depending on quantity purchased)

■ Attribution of impacts to measures: 16 new models were brought to the market, enough to ensure supply capacity. Five manufacturers commercialised new products.

■ Performance improvement: A CFL of smaller size to fit into fixture was developed.

■ Programme cost: 342 000 US$ (for research and preparations, no incentives given)

Remark: This very inexpensive technology procurement programme was highly successful in facilitating the development of modified products and their uptake. It involved the conscious building of relations across the product distribution chain.

18. Clean Coal Technology Demonstration, United States

Diagnosis of measures needed: The operational objective is to manifest and aggregate demand for a complex product used in energy conversion systems.

Match of measures to policies: The measures are in complete harmony with the diagnosis. The challenge has been to define operational targets for the technology issues to be solved and to adjust these targets not only to the technical needs but also to the changing conditions of the market framework. This is underlined by the clear indication of measures that relate to system conditions.

Results:

- Volume growth: Forty projects in 18 states have reached completion.

- Volume and price/cost: Cheap low-NOx burners have been developed.

- Performance improvement: AFBC plants developed; IGCC and PFBC with 20-40% lower CO_2 emissions. Methods to up-grade low-ranked coal developed and commercialised.

- Programme cost: 5.6 BUS$ of which 1/3 was financed by Federal government funds.

Remark: The project illustrates how commercialisation can be achieved when industry responds to challenges made manifest by the government and technology users. It presents an interesting model for government-industry collaboration.

19. Industrial Assessment Center Program (IAC), United States

Run by the Office of Industrial Technologies, USDOE Office of Renewable Energy and Energy Efficiency

Diagnosis of measures needed: This programme is totally focused on customer service.

Match of measures to policies: The measures are primarily on customer service, but with some elements also of consumer protection and the vitalisation of business.

Results:

- Volume and price/cost: The establishment of databases and the tracking of audits/measures, as well as the high degree of implementation (50%), make a positive learning experience highly likely.

- Attribution of impacts to measures: Typically plant managers implement about 50% of the recommendations for measures that will start saving energy immediately.

- Performance improvement: A benefit/cost ratio of 8.1:1 was calculated for measures implemented in 1999.

- Programme cost: Annual budget 8.3 MUS$

- Estimates of energy savings and related impacts due to programme: Annual savings 40.7 MUS$ (app. 55 000 US$ per assessment), 1999 (composed of 9.7 MUS$ for energy, 6.6 MUS$ for waste and 24 MUS$ for productivity).

Remark: This is a strategic and well-conceived model for building a capacity for long lasting results. It involves very important side-effects relating to productivity, waste management, education and customer motivation.

20. Motor Challenge and BestPractices Programs, United States

Diagnosis of measures needed: The case study description indicates that the aggregated volume of demand is too low to provide a basis for the use of higher-performance motors.

Match of measures to policies: The measures taken do not focus directly on aggregating demand, but on providing service that will allow customers to make more educated choices.

Results:

- Volume growth: Over 10 000 purchases of premium motors.

- Volume and market penetration: The volume represents 6% of the market for premium motors.

- Attribution of impacts to measures: 10-15 % of customers implement measures that result in 6% of the market for premium motors.

- Performance improvement: The programme targets premium performance.

- Estimates of energy savings and related impacts due to programme: 24.9 MUS$ in annual savings 1999 (app. 500 GWh per year).

Remark: This programme involves a comprehensive system across industries and makes deliberate and positive use of business interests. Over a long period in which relationships were built, business and R&D issues have been effectively woven into the programme.

21. EnergyPLUS, European Union

Diagnosis of measures needed: The diagnosis has recognised that the characteristics of refrigerator/freezer technologies have developed beyond what is being communicated in the market; the labelling system is undersized and the competition has been developing towards branding rather than performance.

Match of measures to policies: The limitations of existing communication and incentives have to be overcome; aggregating purchasing power is the tool to use.

Results:

- Volume growth: Not recorded but a promising number of retailers are involved.

- Volume and price/cost: Too early to know, but niche markets identified.

- Performance improvement: Remarkable, improvements in the range of 50 % compared to the best technologies available in the market before this point

- Programme cost: 1 MEuro

Remark: The project is in an early stage and will need more time to mature before results can be observed. However, suppliers and retailers have shown remarkable interest in the early stage of the programme.

22. IEA-SolarPACES START Missions

Diagnosis of measures needed: The diagnosis points at many sorts of problems (customer, business organisation, financing) involved in getting a brand new technology into the market.

Match of measures to policies: The measures that have been given priority are those that relate to manifesting demand and to financing.

Results:

- Volume growth: A 130 MW hybrid (fossil-solar) plant is under way

- Volume and market penetration: Negligible

- Volume and price/cost: Not applicable at this stage

- Attribution of impacts to measures: Direct observation of proximate impacts is possible.

- Performance improvement: Not applicable at this stage

Remark: This programme involves a long lead time before results can be observed. So far the direct results are limited but the concept is interesting nevertheless.

ORDER FORM

IEA BOOKS

Fax: +33 (0)1 40 57 65 59
E-mail: books@iea.org
www.iea.org/books

INTERNATIONAL ENERGY AGENCY

9, rue de la Fédération
F-75739 Paris Cedex 15

I would like to order the following publications

PUBLICATIONS	ISBN	QTY	PRICE	TOTAL
☐ **Creating Markets for Energy Technologies**	92-64-09963-8		€75	
☐ World Energy Outlook 2002	92-64-19835-0		€150	
☐ Energy Policies of IEA Countries – 2002 Review (Compendium)	92-64-19773-7		€125	
☐ Dealing with Climate Change - 2002 Edition	92-64-19841-5		€100	
☐ Distributed Generation in Liberalised Electricity Markets	92-64-19802-4		€75	
☐ Security of Supply in Electricity Markets - *Evidence and Policy Issues*	92-64-19805-9		€100	
☐ Bus Systems for the Future - *Achieving Sustainable Transport Worldwide*	92-64-19806-7		€100	
☐ Experience Curves for Energy Technology Policy	92-64-17650-0		Free PDF	
			TOTAL	

DELIVERY DETAILS

Name _____ Organisation _____

Address _____

Country _____ Postcode _____

Telephone _____ E-mail _____

PAYMENT DETAILS

☐ I enclose a cheque payable to IEA Publications for the sum of $ _____ or € _____

☐ Please debit my credit card (tick choice).   ☐ Mastercard   ☐ VISA   ☐ American Express

Card no: |_|_|_|_|_|_|_|_|_|_|_|_|_|_|_|_|_|

Expiry date: |_|_|_|_|_|_| Signature:

OECD PARIS CENTRE
Tel: (+33-01) 45 24 81 67
Fax: (+33-01) 49 10 42 76
E-mail: distribution@oecd.org

OECD BONN CENTRE
Tel: (+49-228) 959 12 15
Fax: (+49-228) 959 12 18
E-mail: bonn.contact@oecd.org

OECD MEXICO CENTRE
Tel: (+52-5) 280 12 09
Fax: (+52-5) 280 04 80
E-mail: mexico.contact@oecd.org

You can also send your order to your nearest OECD sales point or through the OECD online services: www.oecd.org/ bookshop

OECD TOKYO CENTRE
Tel: (+81-3) 3586 2016
Fax: (+81-3) 3584 7929
E-mail: center@oecdtokyo.org

OECD WASHINGTON CENTER
Tel: (+1-202) 785-6323
Toll-free number for orders:
(+1-800) 456-6323
Fax: (+1-202) 785-0350
E-mail: washington.contact@oecd.org

IEA PUBLICATIONS, 9, rue de la Fédération, 75739 PARIS CEDEX 15
PRINTED IN FRANCE BY STEDI
(61 02 34 1P1) ISBN 92-64-09963-8 - 2003